**CAMBRIDGE**

**SECOND EDITION**

# STUDY *writing*

A course in writing skills for academic purposes

Liz Hamp-Lyons
Ben Heasley

CAMBRIDGE UNIVERSITY PRESS
Cambridge, New York, Melbourne, Madrid, Cape Town, Singapore, São Paulo

Cambridge University Press
The Edinburgh Building, Cambridge CB2 2RU, UK

www.cambridge.org
Information on this title: www.cambridge.org/9780521534963

First published 2006

Printed in the United Kingdom at the University Press, Cambridge

A catalogue record for this publication is available from the British Library

ISBN-13 978-0-521-53496-3
ISBN-10 0-521-53496-8

Photo acknowledgement p 51 bildagentur-online.com/th-foto/Alamy

The authors and publishers are grateful for permission to use the copyright materials
appearing in this book, as indicated in the sources and acknowledgements throughout.
If there are errors or omissions the publishers would be pleased to hear and to make
the appropriate correction in future reprints.

# Contents

**Teaching notes and Key**

# Acknowledgements

We would like to acknowledge the help of Harvey Broadstock, Director of Studies, English Language Institute, Victoria University, Melbourne, Australia, and Eric Glendinning, Director, Institute for Applied Language Studies, University of Edinburgh, Scotland for access to their teachers and students for trials of material for this book; and Libya Charleson and Janet Hamilton at the English Language Institute, Victoria University and Kenneth Anderson at the Institute for Applied Language Studies, University of Edinburgh, for trialling materials with their students and providing us with feedback from the teacher's perspective. We particularly thank Janet Hamilton for her help with editorial commentaries on early units, which helped greatly in working out the structure for the book.

We thank all those we have worked with at CUP over what turned out to be more years than any of us wished! Peter Donovan instigated the idea of new versions of all the books in this series; Mickey Bonin worked with us to get the plans off the ground and provided useful external reviews and comments of his own; Alison Sharpe picked up the project towards the end and provided the kind of forceful encouragement we needed to get to the end. Shirley Whitehouse has been a wonderful editor for the final stages.

We must also thank colleagues who over the years since the original *Study Writing* was published in 1987 have approached us at conferences with words of praise for the book; and more recently, it has been a pleasure to meet academic colleagues – in ELT and other disciplines – who have reported that *Study Writing* was a significant force in helping them write well enough to further their academic careers: these have been the people who provided the impetus we needed to undertake a new edition.

Our families have grown up since 1987, but their role in our lives remains central. Our love and thanks go as always to Mike, Nick and Chris; and to Hilda, Yana, Myles and Cian.

# To the Student

In this section we will outline answers to frequently asked questions. We hope you find them helpful.

**Q: Who is this textbook for?**
We think *Study Writing* is most suitable for students whose English level is between intermediate and early advanced (approximately IELTS 5.0–7.0, 'old' [paper and pencil] TOEFL 480–600, computer-based TOEFL 160–250, or 'new generation' iBT TOEFL 55-100).

Typically you will be adult (17+), be able to write reasonably correct sentences in English, but want to develop your ability to write better academic essays, projects, research articles or theses. Most users of this book will either be going to follow a course of study at an English-medium college or university, or planning to take an examination in English, such as the written paper in IELTS or TOEFL.

**Q: How will the course help me?**
It will help you in five main ways. Firstly, it will introduce you to key concepts in academic writing, such as the role of generalisations, definitions and classifications. Secondly, you will explore the use of information structures such as those used to develop and present an argument, a comparison or a contrast. Thirdly, you will be guided through the language as it is used in academic writing. Fourthly, you will become familiar with particular genres such as the research paper. Finally, you will try out some of the processes which we have found help students to improve their writing abilities, such as how to participate in a virtual peer group and how to get feedback on a piece of writing before you present a final draft.

**Q: Do I need to do anything else, apart from studying this course, in order to improve my writing ability?**
While we sincerely believe that this course will help you become a competent writer, we are the first to acknowledge that there are limits to what a course can achieve. This is because writing is a very complex process involving the ability to communicate in a foreign language (English) and the ability to construct a text that expresses the writer's ideas effectively. The more communicative exposure and practice you can get, the more you will support your progress in writing.

One highly recommended approach to improving your writing is through reading. Specifically, we recommend reading widely in the area of your study/interest. The best way of becoming familiar with the demands of academic writing is to study how other writers meet these demands. For example, if you are unsure of how to use definitions in an academic text it makes sense to see how established writers deal with this issue. We recommend keeping a log book of extracts from readings that strike you as interesting/useful from a writer's point of view. These extracts can highlight a range of items, such as language expressions that can be used to signal support for an argument, or ways of moving from one topic to another.

A more obvious way you can help yourself to improve is by writing regularly. Part of writing ability is skill-based, and like any skill it gets better with practice. Even writing that nobody reads except yourself is good practice, helping you to think about ideas and how to express them. But especially important is attending to any feedback that you get on your writing. Without attention to feedback, improvement will not take place. You and other learners can discuss the ideas and arguments in each other's writing and learn a lot from that; you can give written feedback to each other on how effective you find each other's texts (we don't advise you to try to correct each other's language though!) Your teachers will provide you with feedback on language errors, but also on content, organisation and style. In engaging with different kinds of feedback you will improve the quality of your writing in terms of grammar, vocabulary choice, organisation and content.

## To the Teacher

*Study Writing* is designed for students whose English level is between intermediate and early advanced (approximately IELTS Band 5.0–7.0, 'old' [paper and pencil] TOEFL 480–600, computer-based TOEFL 160–250, or 'new generation' iBT TOEFL 55-100). Typically they will be adult (17+), be able to write reasonably correct sentences in English, but want to develop their ability to write better academic essays, projects, research articles or theses. Students will most likely either be going to follow a course of study at an English-medium college or university, or planning to take an examination in English, such as the written paper in IELTS or TOEFL.

### Timing

While the course provides between 40 and 60 hours of classwork, it is not advisable for every task to be undertaken in class time. Many tasks will be more appropriate for homework, for example researching on the World Wide Web or writing long texts. In general, we have erred on the side of providing too many rather than too few tasks, giving considerable flexibility to teachers in how they manage the course and respond to the needs of the students.

### General principles

*Study Writing* is based on an approach which emphasises the discoursal and cognitive aspects of writing. We see writing as a form of problem-solving in which the writer is faced with two main tasks: a) generating ideas, and b) composing these ideas into a written text that meets the needs of a reader and efficiently communicates the author's message. In generating ideas we promote group work, brainstorming and visualisations such as clustering. In transforming these ideas into a written form we guide students in exploring the use of information structures such as generalisations, definitions, the use of Situation–Problem–Solution–Evaluation, and the Introduction–Method–Results–Discussion structure used in research papers. We also stress the value of being attentive to how other, more established writers meet the demands of academic writing. We recommend that students keep a log book of extracts from readings that strike them as interesting and useful from a writer's point of view. These extracts can highlight a range of items, such as language expressions that can be used to signal support for an argument, or ways of moving from one topic to another.

We also acknowledge that part of writing ability is skill-based, and like any skill it gets better with practice because it helps students to think about ideas and how to express them. Therefore it makes sense to encourage students to write even if nobody will read what they write. This is not to downplay the provision of feedback to the student. Without attention to feedback, the rate of improvement will be unnecessarily slow. We help students discuss the ideas and arguments in each other's writing and show them how to give written feedback to each other on how effective they find each other's texts. However, it is up to you as teacher to provide feedback on language errors, and also on content, organisation and style. In engaging the student with these different kinds of feedback they will improve the quality of their writing in terms of grammar, vocabulary choice, organisation and content.

The first edition of *Study Writing* had a substantial section on 'Providing feedback on written work'. In the late 1980s, few second-language teachers knew about process approaches to the teaching of writing, and it was useful to provide such support material, but that situation has changed substantially. This edition of *Study Writing* continues to stress the importance of working with others, and of talking about ideas when engaging in a writing activity, but there is much less need to explain how these processes work. We have instead provided an updated and more sophisticated treatment of 'Assessing written work', which we hope will be of use to the modern English language teacher who knows about curriculum and about pedagogy for teaching writing, but may be less confident about assessment. You will find this material in Appendix C.

## Course organisation

Unit 1 provides the student with an overview of the major elements involved in academic writing. They learn to examine and evaluate their own writing processes, to distinguish between academic and personal styles of writing, explore the grammar of academic discourse and begin visualising their texts. Subsequent units build on this foundation and students are guided, on the one hand, towards mastery of increasingly complex information structures and, on the other hand, through strategies (such as peer group review) that help them produce increasingly more complex texts. This development culminates in Unit 10, which deals with the creation of whole texts, the structure of the research report and papers, creating bibliographies and trying to achieve an authorial voice.

## General advice on teaching procedure

The general principles which we outline here are taken from the first edition of *Study Writing* and have, we believe, stood the test of time.

We do not believe that there is a 'right way' to teach writing, and we do believe that individual teachers should be allowed the freedom to make their own decisions. Nevertheless, the writers of a book always have certain ideas and assumptions which necessarily affect the book they write, so that it is easier to use the materials in some ways than others. We state our general views here in the hope that they will be helpful to the teacher seeking to understand why we have done this or that, and how we might teach it: this is not intended as a prescription of how any other teacher should do it.

Writing is clearly a complex process, and competent writing is frequently accepted as being the last language skill to be acquired (for native speakers of the language as well as for those learning a foreign/second language). Few people write spontaneously, and few feel comfortable with a formal writing task intended for the eyes of someone else. When the 'someone else' is a teacher, whose eye may be critical, and who indeed may assign a formal assessment to the written product, most people feel uncomfortable. It makes sense, then, that the atmosphere of the writing classroom should be warm and supportive, and non-threatening. It helps if teachers show willingness to write too, and to offer their attempts for class discussion along with those of the students; it helps if students can work together, assisting each other, reviewing each other's texts, pointing out strengths and weaknesses without taking or giving offence. Many of our tasks suggest working with a partner or in groups, and we see this work as very important: not only does it make the task livelier and more enjoyable, but it ensures that students see that writing is really cooperative, a relationship between writer and reader. Usually the writer has to imagine a reader, but cooperative writing provides each writer with a reader and makes the writing task more realistic and more interactive.

Writing is commonly seen as a three-stage process: pre-writing, writing and rewriting. Although this is very much an oversimplification, it is a helpful one. In the past, teachers concentrated on the end of the second stage, that is, after the writing had been done. They did not see how they could intervene at the pre-writing and writing stages, and rewriting was seen only as 'correcting the mistakes'. We now understand the importance of all three stages as part of the writing process and try to help students master the process, by participating in it with them, rather than contenting ourselves with criticizing the *product* – the composition – without knowing much about how it was arrived at.

We have included a *Teaching notes and Key* at the back of the book, for those teachers who would like more detailed guidance on how to use *Study Writing*.

# UNIT 1 The academic writing process

**This unit aims to improve writing skills by:**

1. introducing the idea that writing is a set of processes
2. showing how to distinguish between academic and personal styles of writing
3. looking at the grammar of academic discourse
4. practising visualising text as a pre-writing step.

## Introduction

You will already be capable of writing in English and so this course is intended to extend that skill to include the different types of written English essential for studying.

In this unit, we will show you examples of both personal and formal writing and help you distinguish between them. A number of texts will be used as examples of the writing process, and you will be asked to identify the elements of grammar that indicate formal writing.

In later units, we will study the processes of writing in more detail. All the later units will include opportunities to learn and practise at least one of the key grammatical elements identified here.

## Thinking about writing processes

People set about the writing process in many different ways. They require all kinds of different situations in which to feel 'comfortable' when writing. Use the following short questionnaire to help you think about your own writing processes.

- When you write an important text, do you make more than one draft?
- Do you prefer to write on paper or use a computer? Have you ever asked yourself **why**?
- What do you do before you start writing?
- How do you start writing? Do you begin at 'the beginning' or jump in wherever you have some ideas? Do you think one approach is better than another?
- What do you do while you are writing? Do you stop and think? Do you ever go back to the beginning and start again?
- When you finish your first complete draft, what do you do next?

If you are working with others, choose a partner and discuss your answers to the questionnaire. There are no 'correct' answers, so freely discuss all views. Would your answers be the same for writing in your own language as for writing in English?

Now that you have considered some basic questions about writing, ask yourself:

*What do I hope to get from this course?*

If you are working in a group, your teacher may want you to discuss this question with others. Alternatively, you may be asked to write a **rough draft** of a short answer at home.[1]

## Distinguishing between academic and personal styles of writing

### What is academic writing?

There are many different kinds of academic writing in English. Some of these differences arise from the different disciplines and the ways in which they create and share knowledge; some relate to the audience (the reader); and some to the use to which the text will be put.

The rules of academic writing in English are quite complicated; nevertheless most students find that they can recognise the difference between informal writing and formal, academic writing.

···························

**TASK 1** *Recognising academic writing*

**A:** Look at the following sentence.

*Linguists were and remain convinced by Noam Chomsky of the Massachusetts Institute of Technology, who discovered that however disparate human languages seem, all share a common, basic structure, seemingly hardwired into the brain.*

If you are working in a group, choose a partner and together identify at least three features of this sentence that you think are **academic**.

**B:** Now look at the following sentence.

*The way you speak says a lot about you.*

---

1 A rough draft is a first version of a piece of writing: it might be early thinking about a topic for an essay or report; or, **as in this case**, it might be a way of capturing your thinking about something in order to talk clearly about it later.

With your partner, identify at least three features of this sentence that seem non-academic to you.

**Note:** This separation between academic and non-academic is not simple or absolute. You will see non-academic style in academic texts; and academic features will occur in non-academic texts. But it is generally true that academic texts have predictable patterns of grammar, organisation, argument, and of giving credit to the work and words of others. You will learn about these predictable patterns in this book.

**TASK 2** *Recognising levels of formality*

Study Table 1.1, which identifies two quite different levels of formality, and then complete the table that follows.

**Table 1.1**: *Different levels of formality*

|  | Academic | Non-academic |
|---|---|---|
| **Reader** | academics | family and friends |
| **Content** | serious thought | conversational |
| **Style** | complex sentences showing considerable variety in construction | mostly simple and compound sentences joined by conjunctions such as *and* or *but* |
| **Organisation** | clear and well planned | less likely to be as clear and as organised |
| **Grammar** | likely to be error free | may not always use complete sentences |
| **Vocabulary** | technical and academic language used accurately | use of short forms, idioms and slang |

Read the sentences and tick (✓) either F (formal) or I (informal) after each sentence. Make notes on which features helped you reach your decision.

| Sentences | F | I | Notes |
|---|---|---|---|
| I couldn't finish the interviews on time. |  |  |  |
| The initial tests were completed and the results analysed by June 2002. |  |  |  |
| I'd like to start by drawing your attention to previous research in this area. |  |  |  |
| In the 1990s, some researchers started to point out the problems with this theory. |  |  |  |
| He agreed with me that this procedure didn't make much sense. |  |  |  |
| We'll repeat the test sometime next year. |  |  |  |
| While it is still too early to draw firm conclusions from the data, preliminary analysis suggests the following trends are present. |  |  |  |
| In addition, the research attempts to answer two further related questions. |  |  |  |

**TASK 3** *Distinguishing between levels of formality*

Put the following texts in order by giving 1 to the most academic and 4 to the least academic. To help you, think about: Who is this text intended for? Why would readers pick up this text and read it? What resources did the writer of the text have available?

## A

What makes a good paragraph? It's difficult to say. Anyway, I'll try to give you an answer. A good paragraph starts with a main idea of some kind. The rest of the paragraph goes on to develop the main idea by explaining it, or by supporting it with evidence.

## B

The reciprocal relationship between reading and writing has become a focal point of L1 and L2 literacy research. Empirical findings have led researchers to recognize that reading and composing (i.e. writing) both involve the construction of meaning, development and application of complex cognitive and linguistic skills, activation of existing knowledge and past experience, and the ability to solve problems.

## C

The difference between a paper and an online presentation is that in print your document forms a whole and the reader is focused on the entire set of information, whereas on the Web you need to split each document into multiple hyperlinked pages since users are not willing to read long pages.

http://www.sun.com/980713/webwriting/wftw1.html

## D

The University of Aizu was established in April 1993 with the goal of educating and graduating students who would become Japan's leading professionals in computer science and engineering (Kunii, 1994). With this in mind, the University's curriculum has been planned to include courses that will provide its graduates with the ability to effectively communicate in English, the international computer science language. The capability to document scholarly and research activities in a form that can be readily disseminated to the international computer science community is considered to be essential for all scientists and engineers. Effective writing is a necessary skill for technical professionals, and it has been claimed that scientists and engineers spend 25% of their professional time on writing a variety of technically oriented documents (15% informal, and 10% formal) (Huckin, 1991). To prepare our students for these endeavours, a two-term English Technical Writing course has been included in the required curriculum of all University of Aizu students.

**TASK 4** *Explaining features of formality*

Using the features shown in Table 1.1, try to explain why you have put the extracts (in Task 3) in the order you chose. Make some notes to share with a group of classmates or with the teacher.

**TASK 5** *Reflecting on academic writing*

Look back at the Introduction and the 'Thinking about writing processes' section of this unit, and think about your own language. What might your responses have been if you were looking at academic writing in your own language? Make some notes as you go. Then turn your notes into a short piece of writing that would begin to answer the question:

> *Are the rules for academic writing in your native language the same as, or different from, those for writing in English?*

## The grammar of academic discourse

**TASK 6** *Grammatical features of academic writing*

Study Table 1.2, which shows some types of language commonly associated with academic and non-academic writing. The key words and expressions are shown in italics (for example *There's*). Note that individual writers do not always use these 'correctly': some academic writers tend towards informality, while some personal writing can seem quite formal.

**Table 1.2**: *Key attributes of academic and non-academic texts*

| Academic writing | Non-academic writing |
|---|---|
| **Full forms** | **Short forms** |
| There *is* | *There's* |
| The test *did not* show | The test *didn't* show |
| **Connectors** | **Connectors** |
| ▶ The theory appears to provide an explanation for this phenomenon. *However*, this is not the case on a closer examination of the facts. | ▶ I want to go to the cinema, *only* I have to work late. |
| ▶ The experimental design was weak. *Moreover*, the methodology was faulty. | ▶ Because of work, I can't go to London this weekend. *Anyway*, I don't have enough money. |
| **Use of nominal groups (verbs made into nouns)** | **Use of pronouns** |
| *The application (noun) of the results* needs to be carefully considered | *We* need to carefully consider *how we apply* the results. |
| rather than: | |
| We need to carefully consider how we *apply (verb)* the results. | |
| **Use of the passive voice** | **Use of the active voice** |
| In recent years, several analyses of survey data *have been published*. | In recent years, researchers *have published* several analyses of survey data. |
| **Concise vocabulary** | **Informal vocabulary** |
| ... *the focus is on x* | ... *talks about x* |
| *Researchers assumed that* ... | *They thought that* ... |
| **Point of view** | **Point of view** |
| ▶ Objective and impersonal, e.g. *This essay attempts to* ... | ▶ Subjective and personal, e.g. *In my essay I will attempt to* ... |
| ▶ Using qualifying language, e.g. *One possible reason may be* ... | ▶ Asking rhetorical questions, e.g. *How can this be so?* |

One kind of academic writing that you will read frequently is the **abstract**. When an academic article is quite long, an abstract serves as a summary or an overview of it. Some lecturers will ask you to write an abstract of your own work. Read the abstract below, then do the tasks that follow.

# Linguistic relativity

An area of disagreement among experts in the relationship between language and the mind is **linguistic relativity**, also known as the **Sapir–Whorf hypothesis**, the very popular notion that each language, because of its linguistic uniqueness, develops its own ways of thinking about the world. For example, if you agree with this opinion you would say that people from Korea 'think differently' from people from Spain because their languages are so different. Even though this belief is popular in many places, there isn't much proof for it. Even experts who disagree about lots of other things often agree that this idea is wrong (Steinberg 1993; Pinker 1994).

[Source: R. Carter & D. Nunan *The Cambridge TESOL Guide*. Cambridge University Press, p. 84.]

● The underlined parts are examples of non-academic language: put each into the correct column, using Table 1.2 for reference. (Note: Some of them may fit into more than one column.)

| Pronouns | Informal vocabulary | Active verbs | Point of view |
|---|---|---|---|
|  |  |  |  |

● Although the text is non-academic, there are a few elements of academic language use. If you are working in a group, choose a partner and see if you can find three examples of academic language in it.

**TASK 7** *Rewriting for formality*
The following text is written in an informal style. Rewrite it as a more formal text by making changes to the grammar and vocabulary.

## Writing a literature review

The literature review means you have to look critically at all the research that is relevant to your research. Some people think that the review is just a summary but I don't agree. A summary is necessary, but you also need to judge the work, show how it holds together, and show how it relates to your work. What I mean is, you just can't describe a whole paper, you have to select which parts of the research you are going to talk about, show how it fits with other people's research, and how it fits with your work.

**TASK 8** *Rewriting for impersonal style*

The following introduction to a text is written in a personal style. Read it, then answer the questions that follow.

### A Way with Words
#### Do languages help mold[2] the way we think?

*A controversial idea from the 1930s is getting a second look.*
By J.R. Minkel

The way you speak says a lot about you. Your dialect or accent might indicate where you grew up, for instance, while your vocabulary may suggest the type of education you've had. But can the language you use – English, Spanish, Mandarin, etc. – indicate the way you think, or help shape those thoughts?

In the 1930s, American linguist Benjamin Lee Whorf argued persuasively that language did indeed affect thought. For instance, Eskimos, who parse "snow" into at least seven different terms, must find our simplistic way of talking about it unthinkable. While Whorf's views fell out of favor – especially that native language created what amounts to a straitjacket for thought – they weren't forgotten. Now a group of cognitive psychologists has revived the search for the effects of language on the mind, with some provocative results.

Researchers first sought out Whorfian effects in the 1950s, looking at color vocabularies. Some languages chop the spectrum into just two categories of light and dark; others make finer, but not necessarily the same, distinctions. Do these

2 This text is written in American English: in British English this would be spelled mould.

linguistic patterns mean that speakers of separate languages perceive color in different ways? Apparently not. By the 1970s, psychologists concluded that linguistic and perceptual distinctions were independent of one another.

[Extracted from: J. R. Minkel, A Way with Words, *Scientific American* March 25, 2002]

1  Why do you think the writer chooses to begin in this way?
2  Rewrite the introduction to make it appear more objective and impersonal, mainly by making changes to the use of pronouns.
3  Replace the rhetorical question and answer in paragraph 3 with a qualifying statement. (A rhetorical question is one where the person asking makes clear the answer he expects; a qualifying statement is one that adds more detail, makes the discussion more precise.)

## The writing process: Visualising your text

To write texts that are academic, begin by thinking about three key elements: audience, purpose and material. Ask yourself: Who is the text for? Why is the text needed? What resources – what data, evidence, reference material, and so on – have I got that I can use? You should then find it easier to start writing. Looking back at Task 6 might also help.

### Ideas for starting an academic text
The following are some ideas for getting started with developing your own academic text.

● **Start with 'material'.** Make sure you have all your research materials in one place. Read quickly through the texts and use (if permitted) highlighters to indicate material that you think you can use in your own writing. Use one colour highlighter for ideas, another for evidence, and another for arguments. Make sure you use the same colour for the same idea wherever it appears. You'll end up with some related points from different texts. That suggests these are important aspects of the topic. Write one or two rough sentences (don't worry about language correctness at this stage) to state one of the ideas or arguments in your own way. Now move on to do the same with another highlighted area.
● **Start with 'purpose'.** Find out what your text is going to be used for. For example, are you expected to *report* or to *argue*? When you read reports, you will see that they are not written in the same

way as essays or arguments. (We will look at these differences in Unit 2.)

● **Start with 'audience'.** Think about who will read what you have written. How much do they know about the topic? What will *they* use the text for? What kinds of writing are they used to reading?

### TASK 9 *Writing about writing*

Write approximately 500 words describing the difficulties you face (or expect to face) in writing academic essays and articles in English. **Before you start**, if you are studying in a group, talk to one or more classmates about who the audience would be for this text (your teacher? your parents? student readers of a college newsletter?), what material you have to work with (your own experience? what else?), and why it might be worth doing this task well (will it help you plan your strategies for learning to write during this course?).

### TASK 10 *Writing about thinking*

This is a harder task and you should only do this if instructed by your teacher.

Write a 500-word essay that you think fits the expectations of 'academic writing' on the following topic:

> *Do languages help mould the way we think? If we all spoke the same language, would we think in the same way? Discuss the issue using examples, details, and your personal experiences of English and your native language.*

# UNIT 2 Researching and writing

This unit aims to improve writing skills by:

1 exploring ways of organising data, using classifications and displays
2 identifying key aspects of academic text structures
3 showing how best to record internet explorations.

## Recognising categories and classifications

Discovering similarities and differences is something that we do both in academic and non-academic contexts. Academics do this by building systems of categorisation – as do people in everyday life.

Being able to organise ideas and concepts into classes and categories is necessary for thinking, and it gives you a basic tool for academic writing. These classes and categories form the main divisions, followed by sub-categories and sub-classes which are smaller and more closely defined.

**TASK 1** *Identifying categories in a text*
The following text is about the effects of globalisation on old people.
1 Read the text.
2 Underline the category (i.e. the main area/topic covered).
3 Indicate the sub-categories that are presented. Use different highlighter pens, or similar, for each sub-category.

## Being old in the global village

In later life the saying 'no man is an island' becomes truer than ever. Older men and women rely on collective support and this can be divided into three overlapping systems. The first is economic, broadly interpreted to include paid and unpaid work. Wherever pensions are low, restricted to civil servants and the military, or non-existent, work is the main means of support in later life. Some elders, usually men, are able to continue in paid jobs, especially if they can shift to easier work, but most are likely to be doing unpaid work such as farming, childcare or housework – often filling in for family members who work in the formal economy.

The second collective support for older people is the family. It operates as a workplace, a source of food, shelter and emotional support and, in the last resort, as a care provider. Those who have no family and cannot work must rely wholly on the third system, formal collectives – charities and different versions of the welfare state. Welfare in the form of pensions and free healthcare has transformed old age in richer OECD countries and charities ward off destitution for some, but they are not a real safety net.

Each of these three systems is being put at risk by globalisation. The free market capitalism that has accompanied economic globalisation has made rich countries much richer while poor countries have stayed the same or fallen back.

http://www.healthmatters.org.uk/stories/wilson.html retrieved 11/01/03

---

**TASK 2** *Creating a classification*
Organise the following words into one or more categories. Label your category/categories.

| | | |
|---|---|---|
| *Internet* | *chicken burger* | *CD player* |
| *education* | *movie* | *Coca-Cola* |
| *American Express* | *entertainment* | *Playstation* |

**TASK 3** *Explaining the basis of a classification*
Write a short text that describes how the classification you have developed (for Task 2) works. If any words did not fit into your classification, list them and try to explain why they do not fit.

## The language of classification

**TASK 4** *Discovering the language of classification*
Look again at the text in Task 1, and underline the **language** that shows you there is a classification.

**TASK 5** *Exploring the language of classification*

Complete the following grid using these items:

| *according to* | | *kinds* | | *divided* |

*Language used in expressing classification*

| | | types | | |
| | | classes | | |
| There are | two | .......... | of effects | resulting from |
| | | categories | | globalisation. |
| | | sorts | | |
| | | varieties | | |

| | are | | .......... | |
| The effects | may be | classified | on the basis of | |
| | can be | | depending upon | |

| The effects of | may be | grouped | into three main categories. | |
| globalisation | can be | .......... | | |

**TASK 6** *Creating a classification*

Arrange each of the following concepts/general terms into a classification scheme. You can add concepts where you think necessary.

1 global corporation, multinational, local company, business, regional enterprise
2 Buddhism, Islam, Protestantism, Religions, Judaism, Catholicism, Sunni, Shia, Christianity
3 CD player, audio equipment, CDs, speakers, amplifier

**TASK 7** *Writing up a classification*

Write a paragraph describing one of the classifications you created in Task 6.

**TASK 8** *Categories and classifications in visuals*

Look at the extract on the next page, which consists of an introduction after which its detailed information is presented graphically.

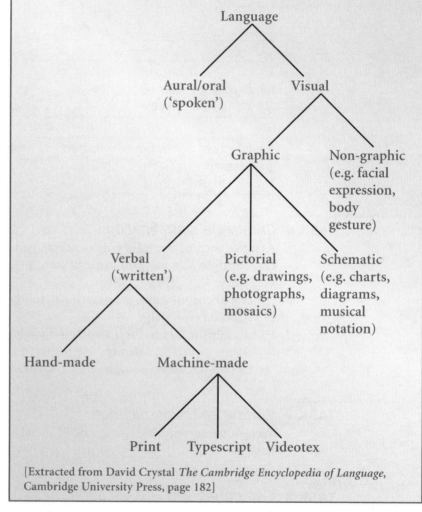

## Modes of graphic expression

The several modes of graphic expression are identified in this diagram, in relation to the study of other kinds of human visual communication and to the linguists' use of the terms 'spoken' and 'written' language. The classification is based on an analysis by the British typographer, Michael Twyman (1934– ), who subsumes all graphic effects under the heading of 'graphic language'.

Language

Aural/oral ('spoken')  Visual

Graphic  Non-graphic (e.g. facial expression, body gesture)

Verbal ('written')  Pictorial (e.g. drawings, photographs, mosaics)  Schematic (e.g. charts, diagrams, musical notation)

Hand-made  Machine-made

Print  Typescript  Videotex

[Extracted from David Crystal *The Cambridge Encyclopedia of Language*, Cambridge University Press, page 182]

Do you think the graphic above is a successful way to present this information? If you are working in a group, choose a partner and try to work out how many sentences it would take to present the same information textually (that is, in writing). Which do you think would be the more successful form of data presentation – graphic or textual?

**TASK 9** *Words or visuals?*

In your pairs, write a verbal version (that is, a version written in words) of the graphic in Task 8. Compare your text with the graphic. Which is the more successful? Why?

**TASK 10** *Creating a graphic*

Read the short extract below and create a graphic display that **categorises** the politeness expressions of English into 10 categories. Add to each category another English expression that fits that category.

---

### Some English politeness formulae

| | |
|---|---|
| *Greetings* | Good morning, Hello, Hi |
| *Farewells* | Good night, Bye, See you, Cheers |
| *Introductions* | How do you do? How's things? Hi |
| *Thanks* | Thank you, Ta, Thanks a lot |
| *Toasts* | Good health, Cheers, Here's to … |
| *Seasonal greetings* | Merry Christmas, Happy Birthday |
| *Apologies* | Sorry, I beg your pardon, My mistake |
| *Response to apologies* | That's OK, Don't mention it, Never mind |
| *Congratulations* | Well done, Right on, Congratulations |
| *Public noises* | Encore, Hear hear, Goal |
| *Body noises* | Excuse me, Bless you, Pardon me |

[Extracted from David Crystal *The Cambridge Encyclopedia of Language*, Cambridge University Press, page 52]

---

**TASK 11** *Working with politeness rules in English*

Complete either part **A** or part **B** below.

**A** Some forms of English (notably, American English) have more etiquette – politeness formulae – than others. If you have any experience with American English you might have noticed that some English politeness formulae have been left out of the diagram above. Preferably with a partner or small group, try to find out what expressions might fit into the categories:

*Response to greetings*   *Reply to introductions*   *Response to thanks*

Now put these categories and their formulaic expressions into the classification diagram you made for Task 10.

**B** Create (with a partner, if possible) a similar graphic that categorises formulaic expressions of politeness **in your own language**.

**TASK 12** *Writing a text*

Now write a text of about 500 words for an international business magazine describing the rules of politeness in your own language.

# The structure of a research paper

In Unit 1, you looked at some common features and patterns of grammar that might lead you to recognise a text as 'academic', one important aspect being the use of a clear and fairly predictable **structure**. By 'structure' we mean the *shape* of the whole text.

Although writers vary in their level of formality, we do expect academic texts to have certain predictable structures. In many academic texts, it is easy to see the organisational structure because it is marked by headings and subheadings.

**TASK 13** *Identifying text structure*

1  If you are working with others, form a small group and identify the **four** most important headings in the outline below. Perhaps start by discussing and agreeing on the top six or seven, then go on to place them in order of importance.
2  Write **one** sentence relating to each of the top four headings explaining why it is important.

**Title: Language learning strategies and EAP proficiency: Teacher views, student views, and test results**

**Introduction**

**Literature Review**

**Method**

   **Subjects**

   Data collection procedure

     1  Learner self-report questionnaire
     2  Teacher questionnaire
     3  Comprehensive proficiency test
     4  Semi-structured interview sheet

   Analysing the data

**Results**

   1  What language learning strategies do City University EAP students use?
   2  Does strategy use differ by discipline?
   3  What strategies are associated with higher or lower levels of proficiency?
   4  What strategies do EAP teachers believe to be the most useful for EAP?
   5  What strategies do EAP students believe to be the most useful for EAP?

**Discussion**

**Conclusion**

[Source: Matthew Peacock *in* J. Flowerdew & M. Peacock (eds) *Research Perspectives on EAP, pp.* 268–285. Cambridge University Press, 2001.]

**TASK 14** *Completing a text structure*

1 Look at the following text, which is the first part of the contents of a World Bank report on globalisation.

**GLOBALIZATION, GROWTH, AND POVERTY: BUILDING AN INCLUSIVE WORLD ECONOMY.**

Contents

2 Now look at the rest of the Table of Contents for this report and match the headings on the left with the subheadings on the right.

[Source: A co-publication of the World Bank and Oxford University Press: http://econ.worldbank.org/files/2895_overview.pdf extracted 18/06/04]

# The writing process: Exploring the Internet and recording your explorations

You have probably known how to use e-mail for some time, but you may not have realised how useful e-mail and other virtual contacts will be to your academic studies. The Internet lets you enter into a virtual community in which all kinds of information and help are available.

**TASK 15** *Using the World Wide Web*

In this task you will navigate the Internet in order to discover a tiny corner of what it has to offer. You will also begin to keep an electronic journal, which will help you record what you discover in your virtual explorations.

1 You will need the URL ('uniform resource locator') of your school or university – ask your teacher for it if necessary. Here are others you might try (please remember that URLs sometimes change):

   http://www.cele.nottingham.ac.uk
   http://owl.english.purdue.edu
   http://ec.hku.hk/elr.asp
   www.wsu.edu/writing programs (you will find some good kinds of writing assistance within this institution's website).

2 Go to the URL you have chosen and explore it to find out the answers to the following questions.

   a) Is there a special unit that teaches English to non-native speakers?

   b) What kinds of courses are offered **specifically** for non-native English speakers?

   c) Is there one or more **writing** courses specifically for non-native speakers? Is there information on what **level** this is/these are?

   d) What **other** writing courses are offered at this institution? Is there information on what levels they teach?

   e) Is there any specialised **individual** help for writers with problems? If so, who is eligible? What services are offered?

3 Use the information you have found in your Internet search to start your e-journal (see Task 16).

**TASK 16** *Writing about what you learn*

You are going to start an 'e-journal' which will be useful to you while you use this book, and which you may find useful enough to keep on using afterwards.

An 'e-journal' is simply an electronic journal – in other words, a journal which is written and stored on the computer. There are many kinds of e-journal and you can design one that suits you. But for this course, you will keep an e-journal in which you write at least once a week.

To begin your electronic journal, carry out the following three steps.

1 Record the explorations you do over the Internet on a specific topic. The first e-journal entry can be a record of where you looked and what you found out for Task 15 above. Copy down the URL and webpage information (and date found) for every source you find useful: look at the way we have done this in this book. But remember that web pages change often, so be sure to note down or print out all the important information you found in that location so you can refer to it later.

2 Don't forget that libraries are still a wonderful resource – in fact, much of your best advice on where to locate electronically-stored information as well as books and periodicals will come from library staff and the search functions your library provides to its physical and virtual holdings. Record the (bibliographic) information about texts you have read in libraries in a similar way: with all the publication/citation information so you can find that text again if you need to, and enough notes to be able to speak/write about what the text's author(s) said. You will probably also want to record your own reactions to what you have read, as well as citation information about any further reading you did as follow-up.

3 Share your e-journal either with your teacher, who **will not** grade or mark it but will make some comments and suggestions, or with a classmate. You can look at it either electronically or on paper. Remember that **talking about what you read and write** is an excellent way to help you remember key ideas.

**TASK 17** *Writing about globalisation*

You have heard in the media and read in more scholarly sources that the world is increasingly 'a global village'. You see this in your own life in the prevalence of universal brands like Coca-Cola and McDonald's, and you know there are world-wide political and economic structures like the World Bank and the United Nations. **Describe some aspects of globalisation that impact on your own life**. Write about 500 words.

Some suggestions for categories to include in your description:

- global <u>mass media</u>
- <u>employment</u> in your country
- the growth of <u>world music</u>
- the <u>World Wide Web</u>.

This piece of writing is going to be evaluated by your teacher.

# UNIT 3 Fundamentals and feedback

This unit aims to improve your writing skills by:

1. exploring alternative text structures to use when comparing and contrasting
2. looking at the language of comparison and contrast
3. showing how comparisons and contrasts can lead on to evaluations and recommendations
4. practising assessing and evaluating claims made in research papers
5. showing you how to get feedback on your writing via a virtual peer group.

## Exploring comparison and contrast structures

When there are two or more bodies of knowledge, theories, arguments or other content, it is useful to compare those aspects that are similar and contrast those that differ. You can use either of two structures to do this effectively in academic writing.

One way is to group all the ideas about Topic A in one section or paragraph, and all the ideas about Topic B in another. The reader then has to recognise the relationship (comparison or contrast) implicit in the two sections. This writing structure is called the AAA–BBB pattern and is illustrated in Figure 3.1.

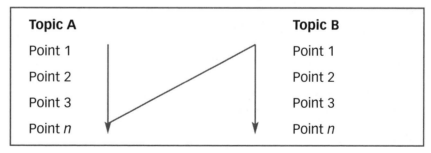

**Figure 3.1: The AAA–BBB pattern**

Another way is to organise the ideas in pairs and then compare and contrast one with the other. The reader can then quickly recognise what is being compared or contrasted. This writing structure is called the AB–AB–AB pattern and is illustrated in Figure 3.2.

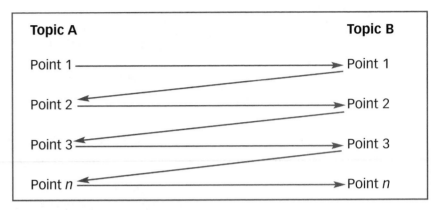

Topic A | Topic B

Point 1 → Point 1
Point 2 → Point 2
Point 3 → Point 3
Point *n* → Point *n*

**Figure 3.2: The AB–AB–AB pattern**

The pattern you use for an academic piece of writing will depend on your preference, the text you are writing and your purpose in writing it.

**TASK 1** *Identifying patterns in texts*

To practise recognising the different structures, read Texts 1–3 and decide which patterns they follow (AAA–BBB or AB–AB–AB).

---

**Text 1**

In the strict botanical sense, the term 'fruit' applies to the structure, usually containing seeds, which develops from the flowery ovary after pollination and fertilization. In the food sense, fruits are succulent structures (with seeds or seedless) exhibiting a pleasant aroma and flavour. There are many fruit species, showing a range of habits (herbaceous, shrubby, and tree-like) and coming from a variety of families, although two families, namely the Rosaceae (apple, pear, plum, strawberry, and others) and the Rutaceae (orange, lemon, grapefruit, and others) are of outstanding importance. It is difficult to define the culinary term 'vegetable'. Vegetables (and salad plants) are edible plant products which can be modified stems (e.g. potato), roots (e.g. cassava) leaves (e.g. cabbage), and even fruits in the scientific sense (e.g. tomato). Normally vegetables are not sweet and are usually eaten with meat, fish, or savoury dishes.

[Extracted from: Vaughan, J.G. and C. Geissler (1997) *The New Oxford Book of Food Plants.* Oxford: Oxford University Press. (p. xviii)]

**Text 2**

The difference between a spice and a herb is not always easy to define, but in general terms, spices can originate from various parts of a plant body (seeds, fruits, bark, roots) and they tend to originate in semi-tropical climates. On the other hand, herbs are the leafy parts of soft-stemmed plants and are found in more temperate regions.

[Extracted from: Vaughan, J.G. and C. Geissler (1997) *The New Oxford Book of Food Plants*. Oxford: Oxford University Press. (p. xix)]

**Text 3**

There are many points of comparison between plant and animal organ systems. The plant's roots absorb water and nutrients just as the animal digestive system does. The roots also anchor the plant to keep it from moving, but there is no comparable internal animal system. Stems provide support for the plant as the skeletal system does for animals. The stems also transport water to the leaves and sugar to the roots; the circulatory system performs a similar function for animals.

[Adapted from http://www.specialedprep.net/MSAT%20SCIENCE/ComparisonPlantAnim.htm]

**TASK 2** *Identifying category features*

1 Reread Text 1 and complete the following grid by adding '+' or '–', as appropriate, for **stereotypical** fruits and vegetables used in your culture. (The first one has been done for you: it shows that your culture's fruits sometimes do contain seeds, sometimes not.)

| Feature | Fruits | Vegetables |
|---|---|---|
| Contain seeds | +/– | |
| Pleasant smell | | |
| Sweet taste | | |

2 Now write two sentences: one containing a comparison and one containing a contrast between your culture's fruits and vegetables.

**TASK 3** *Creating categories*

Reread Text 2 about spices and herbs. Then, on the next page list some examples of spices and herbs that you use in your country. Use this list to help you compare dishes from your country or region with those of another. List both the name of each dish and its key ingredients.

|  | From your country or region | From another country or region |
| --- | --- | --- |
| Spices and herbs |  |  |
|  |  |  |
|  |  |  |
|  |  |  |

⋮

**TASK 4** *Completing comparisons*

The following extract compares food prices in the United States with those in the European Union. Complete the text using these expressions:

> *lower    somewhat more expensive    are different from*
> *wealthier    cost    difference    much higher*
> *generally of lower quality    costing    comparing*
> *would cost    higher*

Many foods are less expensive in the United States than in the …. (1) …. countries of the EU, but food is …. (2)…. in the United States than in the less wealthy countries of the EU. Both the EU and the United States have …. (3) …. food prices than the wealthiest Eastern European countries, with the exception of Slovenia. One problem with …. (4) …. purchasing power parity from country to country, or even within the EU or the United States, is that qualitative differences might be difficult to capture. Meat is …. (5) …. in Eastern Europe. Products available vary within the United States from region to region, and …. (6) …. those available in the EU. Thus, some of the price differences might be capturing differences in quality. Table 3.1 gives purchasing power parity indices for food prices in the countries considered here. A quantity of bread and cereal items that …. (7) …. $100 in the United States would cost $156 in Denmark, but only $85 in Portugal, and only $40 in the Czech Republic. Meat costs are …. (8) …. in most EU countries than in the United States, but are much …. (9) …. in the Eastern European countries. A quantity of meat …. (10) …. $100 in the United States would cost $210 in Denmark, but would only cost $73 in Hungary or Poland. Food prices not only vary between the United States and the EU, but there is remarkable variation within the EU and the United States. Using Sweden as an average (100), the food price index in the EU ranges from 109 in Denmark to 65 in the UK and Portugal, a 68 percent …. (11)….. . This means that a balanced basket of food, representing the consumption of the average person, that costs $65 in the UK, …. (12) …. $109 in Denmark. This price variation is mirrored in the United States. A basket of groceries that cost $141.50 in Manhattan would cost $93.30 in Houston, a difference of 52 percent.

[Extracted from http://www.ers.usda.gov/publications/WRS0404/WRS0404f.pdf on 17/10/03]

# The language of comparison and contrast

**TASK 5** *Writing comparison and contrast sentences*

Compare five countries from Table 3.1 with respect to their GNP, bread and cereal, and meat index. Use the language summaries shown in Table 3.2 to help you.

*Table 3.1: Incomes and food prices*

| Country | 1998 GNP per capita (constant 1995 $US) | Average growth rate of GNP per capita, 1994–98 | Bread and cereal price index 1998 (PPP) | Meat Price index 1998 (PPP) |
|---|---|---|---|---|
| **United States** | 29,316 | 2.66 | 100 | 100 |
| **EU** | | | | |
| Austria | 30,841 | 2.21 | 114 | 163 |
| Belgium | 29,284 | 2.36 | 116 | 161 |
| Denmark | 36,892 | 3.30 | 156 | 210 |
| Finland | 27,807 | 5.23 | 147 | 156 |
| France | 28,028 | 2.19 | 125 | 157 |
| Germany | 30,941 | 1.65 | 145 | 187 |
| Greece | 12,111 | 2.32 | 104 | 102 |
| Ireland | 19,469 | 7.78 | 80 | 103 |
| Italy | 19,363 | 1.68 | 101 | 135 |
| Luxembourg | 50,851 | 1.22 | NA | NA |
| Netherlands | 28,344 | 2.81 | 106 | 176 |
| Portugal | 11,573 | 2.82 | 85 | 116 |
| Spain | 15,405 | 2.66 | 89 | 91 |
| Sweden | 26,613 | 2.34 | 151 | 179 |
| United Kingdom | 20,214 | 2.72 | 90 | 128 |

[Extracted from http://www.ers.usda.gov/publications/WRS0404/WRS0404f.pdf on 17/10/03]

*Table 3.2 Examples of language to use when comparing and contrasting*

| Comparison within sentences | Contrast within sentences |
|---|---|
| A is like B<br>A and B are similar<br>A is similar to B          with respect to cost<br>A resembles B | A is unlike B<br>A differs from B<br>A and B differ          with respect to cost<br>A is different from B<br>A contrasts with B |
| Both A and B cost $100.<br>A is as costly as B.<br>A is no more expensive than B.<br>A costs the same as B. | A costs $100 whereas B costs $150.<br>A costs $100 while B costs $150.<br>A costs $100, but B costs $150.<br>B costs more than A.<br>A is not as expensive as B. |

**TASK 6** *Making comparisons and contrasts between sentences*
Comparisons and contrasts can be contained in sentences – or pairs of sentences – as well as paragraphs and sections. Put sentences 1–6 under the correct heading below. The first one has been done for you.

1 A is expensive to buy. Similarly, it is expensive to operate.
2 A is expensive to buy. On the other hand, it is cheap to operate.
3 A is expensive to buy. In contrast, it is cheap to operate.
4 A is expensive to buy. Correspondingly, it is expensive to operate.
5 A is expensive to buy. Conversely, it is cheap to operate.
6 A is expensive to buy. Likewise, it is expensive to operate.

| Comparison between sentences | Contrast between sentences |
| --- | --- |
| 1, | |

**TASK 7** *Writing a text containing contrasts*
The following table contrasts two kinds of coffee plants: Arabica coffee and Robusta coffee. Use the information in the table to write a text contrasting the two types. Imagine you are writing the text as part of an entry for an encyclopaedia. If you are working in a group, your teacher will ask some of you to write the text using an AAA–BBB plan and some of you to use an AB–AB–AB plan.

| Category | Arabica | Robusta |
| --- | --- | --- |
| Origin | South western highlands of Ethiopia | African equatorial forests |
| Commercially grown in | Central and South America (especially Brazil), Kenya and Tanzania | West Africa, Uganda and Indonesia |
| Where cultivated | High altitudes | Lower altitudes |
| Height | 5 metres | 10 metres |
| Caffeine content | 1–1.5 per cent | 2–2.5 per cent |
| Quality | superior | inferior |
| Price | most expensive | less expensive |

**TASK 8** *Deciding on the most appropriate pattern*
Find a partner who has a different version (of Task 7 answer) to yours. Discuss which of your versions you think would be the best for an encyclopaedia. Note your reasons as they may help you later in this course, or in real-life academic writing situations.

............................
**TASK 9** *Writing a text of comparisons or a questionnaire*
Read the article below, which is from a popular newspaper and gives specific advice to British people on how to improve their health. Ask yourself: How do my habits compare to those recommended here? Then answer either question 1 or 2.

## Top ten healthy habits

1 Drink about 2 litres of water per day. Apart from contributing to general wellbeing, drinking more water has been associated with substantially reduced risk of heart disease and certain cancers. Keep a bottle at hand.

2 Eat more fruit. Fruit is packed with health-giving substances. One study found that increasing fruit consumption by only 50g (about half an apple) each day might reduce risk of premature death by 20 per cent.

3 Eat more fat. Not all fat is bad. Some fats in the diet, such as those found in oily fish, extra virgin olive oil, nuts, seeds and avocado, have positive healthy giving properties. Eating foods rich in healthy fat can stave off all sorts of conditions including heart disease, some cancers and depression.

4 Eat whole-grains. Compared to their refined counterparts, whole-grains contain more fibre, are more nutritious and give more sustained releases of sugar into the bloodstream too.

5 Eat between meals. Although we have been advised not to eat between meals, the evidence suggests that healthy snacking can actually help weight loss and reduces cholesterol levels. Contrary to popular opinion, eating healthy snacks such as fresh fruit and the odd handful of raw nuts seems to be beneficial for health in the long term.

6 Take a multivitamin and mineral. Recent evidence shows that a significant proportion of men eat diets deficient in vitamins A and C, calcium, magnesium and zinc, while women tend to go short on vitamins A and C, folic acid, calcium magnesium, zinc, copper and iron and iodine. Taking a decent multivitamin and mineral each day ensures you'll get all the nutrients you need.

7 Get walking. Regular exercise has been associated with a range of health benefits including reduced blood pressure, stronger bones and better mood, plus a lower risk of heart disease and diabetes.

8 Breathe deeply. Proper breathing ensures we have enough oxygen to supply the body's cell. Just 10 or 15 deep breaths into the stomach, two or three times a day, can often boost physical and mental energy.

9 Treat yourself. Stress in excess has been linked with an assortment of ailments. Massage, aromatherapy or other stress relieving treatments may help dissipate stress.

10 Get out more. Sunlight exposure has important mood enhancing effects. Getting out in the light each day can help recharge the batteries.

[Adapted from the *Observer Food Monthly*. January 2003. No 22]

1 Write a text comparing your lifestyle with the top ten healthy habits mentioned in the article. Imagine you are writing the text for a nutritional consultant your doctor is sending you to. Before you begin, decide which pattern would be the most appropriate: the AAA–BBB or the AB–AB–AB pattern.

2 If you are working in a large group, form a smaller group and create a questionnaire based on the article. Administer the questionnaire to the large group and, in pairs, write up a report. Keep your report because, later on, you will be asked to add a section containing your recommendations on how to improve the class's lifestyle.

### Using comparisons and contrasts to evaluate and recommend

Usually when we are comparing and contrasting two or more things, we also have to evaluate which one is the best or most appropriate for a particular purpose. We do this by measuring the item against generally accepted concepts, such as quantity, cost, and so forth.

**TASK 10** *Creating evaluation categories*

What categories might we use to compare and contrast foods in the shops? Add five more categories to this list.

> *Quantity*
> *Cost*
> ...............
> ...............
> ...............
> ...............
> ...............

**TASK 11** *Identifying evaluation categories/concepts*

Read texts **A** to **C**. If you are working in a group, choose a partner and together decide what concepts/categories the writers have used in their evaluations (in the same way that we used 'cost', for example, as a concept/category for comparing and contrasting food in Task 10).

---

**Text A**

The survey showed that more students (80%) preferred to eat French fries than boiled potatoes (5%) or rice (10%). However, given that French fries are not a healthy option owing to their excessive fat content, we need to try to reverse this trend.

**Text B**

There are few issues in life that are clear cut and it would be foolish to pretend that modern farming practices do not impose some costs. But these must be set against the benefits they deliver. In my 20 years of experience with food and farming, the supermarkets have broadened the range of choice for consumers while forcing the food chain to improve quality and hygiene.

**Text C**

In 1970 the average household in Britain spent 26% of its income on food compared with around 15% today (2001). This is a very real benefit, particularly for those households where incomes are low ...

[Adapted from: Is there a crisis in British farming? *Prospect*: Issue 62, April 2001]

**TASK 12** *Writing a text with an evaluation*

Study the following matrix, which shows the desirable and undesirable effects of some of the developments in food technology in the last fifty years or so. Write a 250-word text with the title:

*Evaluating trends in convenience foods*

|  | Innovation | Long-term effects | |
|---|---|---|---|
|  |  | desirable | undesirable |
| a) | Fast-food restaurants | cheap meals | bad effects on health |
| b) | Genetically modified food | more food can be produced because crops are protected from diseases | little known about the long-term effects on people and the environment |
| c) | Pre-cooked meals | no preparation required, quick to cook | people will lose the ability to cook for themselves, all meals will taste the same |

TASK 13  *Completing the text*

Complete the short paragraph using these words:

*evaluates    evaluations    recommendations*

> Recommendations usually follow …(1)…, often in the next
> paragraph. If a writer compares a number of items and …(2)…
> one of them as outstanding, we would expect that …(3)… will
> also be made regarding who it is to be used by, in what
> circumstances, etc.

TASK 14  *Identifying the language of recommendation*

Read this extract from a report by The Royal Society on 'Genetically
Modified Plants for Food Use', and underline the words that signal a
recommendation. (In the article, GM stands for 'genetically
modified' and GMO for 'genetically modified organism'.)

We strongly support mechanisms by which consumers can be informed about developments in biotechnology, including the labelling of foods containing GM material where the equivalence of a food is substantially changed, according to established criteria and provided such labelling is appropriately monitored. Nevertheless, we recognise the associated practical problems, whether related to the complexity of international trade, detection limits, complexity of product formulations or processing techniques. We recommend that the Government departments continue to work with the European Commission and all interested parties towards increased clarity in the labelling regulations. To ensure labelling is possible, the regulatory authorities will also need to analyse information exchange throughout the supply chain for GM food products.

The reliance on a case-by-case approach to the legislation may result in a lack of analysis of the overall impact of the technology on agriculture and the environment, and of the long-term effects of GMOs. We therefore recommend that the remit of the appropriate advisory committees should be extended to include, where relevant, the following points. In addition, an over-arching body or 'super-regulator' should be commissioned by the Government to span departmental responsibilities and have an ongoing role to monitor the wider issues associated with the development of GM plants. Such a body should consider those of the following points which cannot be considered by individual advisory committees for practical reasons. In addition, the proposed Food Standards Agency might have a role to play.

[The Royal Society (September 1998) Genetically modified plants for food use.
http://www.royalsoc.ac.uk/templates/statements/statementDetails.cfm?StatementID=56 Extracted 07/02/03]

# The research paper

In undertaking research, the researcher needs to: 1) map out a field of research then 2) find a research space – a **gap** in the research that needs to be filled.

**TASK 15** *Identifying the language used to map out the research field*

The grid below shows three ways of mapping out a field of research. Put each of the example sentences (1–10) under one of these three ways. The first one is done for you.

| **claiming** that the research to be undertaken is central to the area | **making generalisations** about a topic | reviewing **items of previous research** |
| --- | --- | --- |
| **1**, | | |

1  *Recently there has been a spate of interest in how …*
2  There are many situations where …
3  The study of … has become an important aspect of …
4  The aetiology and pathology of … is well known.
5  Although [A, B and C] have claimed that …, their own data do not support that conclusion.
6  A standard procedure for assessing has been …
7  The effect of … has been studied extensively in recent years.
8  … is a common finding in patients with …
9  In recent years, applied researchers have become interested in …
10  There is now much evidence to support the hypothesis that …

**TASK 16** *Identifying the language used to show a research gap*

The following categories are four ways of finding a research gap. Put each of the example clauses (on page 46) under one of these four ways. The first one is done for you.

| **claiming** that there is a gap in the previous research | **making a counter-claim** (i.e. claiming that previous work in this research area was wrong) | **raising a question** about a theory, previous research, etc. | **continuing a tradition** |
| --- | --- | --- | --- |
| | | | **1**, |

1 *One would intuitively expect* …
2 The differences need to be analysed …
3 Both [currently held views] suffer from the dependency on …
4 The first group … cannot treat … and is limited to …
5 A question remains whether this line of enquiry is valid.
6 If there really is other intelligent life in the universe, why hasn't it contacted us?
7 However, the previously mentioned methods fail to take account of …
8 Research in the area of [xxxx] is long overdue.
9 It is of interest to compare the work of [A with B].
10 It has been predicted that life could spontaneously arise inside a black hole. However, this is impossible because …
11 Studies in 'writing assessment' [A; B; etc.] have shown that … This study extends the work of [A and B] to ask …

[Many of the examples from Tasks 15 and 16 are taken or adapted from J.M. Swales, 1990. *Genre Analysis*. Cambridge University Press: Ch. 7]

**TASK 17** *Recognising how a research field is mapped out*
Read the following text, which introduces an investigation of the food intakes and preferences and other factors influencing dietary adequacy among old people in hospitals in Malaysia. If you are working in a group, choose a partner and discuss the question that follows; if not, simply read the question and write down your response.

*Food intakes and preferences of hospitalised geriatric patients*

## Background

Ageing is related to the deterioration of physiological and health functions, thus, elderly people are more susceptible to various diseases and illnesses. Nutrition plays an important role in preventing diseases and promoting recovery from illnesses. Besides diseases and hospital environment, food preferences are also main factors affecting the food intake of geriatric patients. Thus, hospital menus should be planned according to the preferences of geriatric patients to ensure that they eat what is served to them. Studies on food intakes and habits among Malaysian elderly living in rural areas reported that although the subjects had regular meal patterns, the dietary intake was inadequate. Most of the studies conducted among hospitalised elderly people in Western countries and Malaysia reported that malnutrition (as assessed using anthropometric and biochemical indicators) is common.

With respect to food preferences, elderly people are more likely to stick to their traditional food rather than try new food products. However, some elderly people may change their food preferences due to health reasons and food belief. Ageing is associated with a shift from a diet high in calories, sugar and meat to a diet rich in fruits and vegetables. However, avoidance of certain fruits and vegetables due to food beliefs has been reported in a proportion of rural elderly Malays.

It appeared that there was a need to investigate the adequacy of dietary intake and food preferences among our hospitalised geriatric patients. Therefore, this study aimed to investigate the food intakes and preferences and also factors influencing dietary adequacy among hospitalised geriatric patients. The study was also undertaken as a basis for improving the nutrient intake of patients in order to accelerate recovery from disease and hopefully to reduce the length of a hospital stay.

[Extracted from http://www.biomedcentral.com/147-2318/2/3 on 13/9/03]

1 In the text, in what way(s) do the authors map out the research field? Do they do it by:
   a) claiming that the research to be undertaken is central to the area?
   b) making a generalisation about the topic?
   c) reviewing items of previous research?

2 If more than one method has been used, in what order did they appear?

TASK 18  *Recognising a research gap*

1 In the previous text (Task 17), underline the sentence that refers to a research gap.
2 How is the gap created? Is it by:
   a) making a counter-claim?
   b) indicating a gap in the previous research?
   c) raising a question?
   d) continuing a tradition?

**TASK 19** *Making a reasonable claim?*

Given what we know – about an adequate dietary intake and the role of food preferences in determining our food intake and hence our health – does the underlined statement represent a reasonable claim?

> It appeared that there was a need to investigate the adequacy of dietary intake and food preferences among our hospitalised geriatric patients. Therefore, this study aimed to investigate the food intakes and preferences and also factors influencing dietary adequacy among hospitalised geriatric patients. <u>The study was also undertaken as a basis for improving the nutrient intake of patients in order to accelerate recovery from disease and hopefully to reduce the length of a hospital stay.</u>
>
> [Extracted from http://www.biomedcentral.com/147-2318/2/3 on 13/9/03]

In this section we have illustrated how to:
1  map out a field of research
2  find a research space – a gap in the research that needs to be filled.

The writing of research papers will be further developed in subsequent units.

## The writing process: Joining a virtual peer group to get feedback on your writing

One of the great strengths of the World Wide Web is the way it lets you share your learning with others. The simplest way of doing this is by using e-mail. When you find someone you feel connected with, you can use that connection over distance and time through e-mail, to get and give comments on the writing you do.

**TASK 20** *Writing a text and getting 'virtual peer' feedback*

Steps 1 to 5 outline one way to become part of a virtual peer group. If you are working in a group, discuss this procedure with classmates, evaluate its benefits and drawbacks, and agree whether you will try it out. If you decide not to try it, you will need to work out a different procedure for yourselves. (There will be other feedback ideas in later units.) Then go on to answer questions 1 to 3.

**Step 1** Decide what type of **feedback** you want: do you need some fresh ideas? Some comments on your language? Some response to your arguments? Make notes about what you would most like your reader – your e-mail correspondent – to pay attention to as she or he reads your draft writing.

**Step 2** Turn your notes into a small number of short and clear questions you would like your partner to answer.

**Step 3** Write a short and polite e-mail message to your peer, asking her or him for help.

**Step 4** Copy your list of questions into the e-mail, under your message.

**Step 5** Attach your draft text (the one on which you want feedback) to the message.

1 Write about 500 words on the question of teenagers' food preferences. You will find plenty of source material on the World Wide Web (some websites are suggested below); you should also talk to your fellow students or other younger university/college/senior high school students. Evaluate the advice you find and make recommendations based on your evaluation.

2 Now send your draft to 1–3 peers (fellow students, classmates or other people whose judgements you trust), and get their feedback.

3 Rewrite your text after evaluating the feedback you receive.

## Useful websites:

http://www.fda.gov/
*This is the US Government Food and Drug Administration website.*

http://www.fda.gov/bbs/topics/ANSWERS/2001/ANS01087.html
*For a very radical solution to obesity!*

http://food.oregonstate.edu
*A good source of food advice.*

http://www.bbc.co.uk/health/fitness/food.shtml
*The BBC homepage – lots of good things here!*

# UNIT 4
# Definition, vocabulary and academic clarity

This unit aims to improve writing skills by:
1. introducing the Clarity Principle
2. looking at different types of definitions
3. illustrating when to use definitions and how to structure them
4. showing how academic vocabulary improves texts.

## The Clarity Principle

When we write we have to remember that our readers may not always understand the meaning of the more specialised words and expressions we wish to use. In writing in English we try to predict what readers need, so as to produce clear texts for them. You will learn as you do your academic work that the **Clarity Principle** is taken very seriously in English academic writing. The Clarity Principle states that **a writer should make everything clear to the reader** he or she has in mind. In terms of academic writing, 'the reader' is the particular academic community the writer is addressing.

Definitions are the basic tool for ensuring clarity in referring to concepts. Definitions are important because whenever we write – and especially when we write academic texts – we must be clear.

You learned about grouping and classifying in Unit 2, and in Unit 3 you learned about comparing and contrasting. Both these components of writing skill are extremely useful when it comes to writing definitions, and they are organisational tools that help you to put the Clarity Principle into practice.

**TASK 1** *Understanding what definitions are*

Look at the definitions below: the columns show you the **structure** of the definitions. Each entry in the left-hand column shows what is being defined. Can you find the definition which is factually *incorrect?*

| Concept | 'be' verb | A/an/the | Class/category | 'wh-word' + defining information |
|---------|-----------|----------|----------------|----------------------------------|
| A doctor | is | a | person | who is qualified to treat medical problems. |
| A hospital | is | a | place | where ill people go to receive medical treatment. |
| A disease | is | an | illness | that has a set of characteristic symptoms doctors can recognise. |
| AIDS | is | a | disease | that affects a very small number of people each year. |
| Patients | are | — | people | who are receiving medical treatment. |

Defining concrete terms is usually relatively easy. Such terms as 'thermometer', 'stethoscope' and 'prosthetic' may be unfamiliar to you, but if you look them up in a dictionary you will find an explanation that you can easily turn into a *formal definition* if you follow this simple structure:

*Concept*        *class*            *special feature(s).*
⇩   *is a (form of)*   ⇩      *which*        ⇩
………   *(species of)*   ………               ……… .

**TASK 2**  *Writing definitions*

1 Use the simple structure above to write definitions of these terms/concepts (some everyday and some less common) from the field of health education.
   a) Fitness
   b) Cholesterol
   c) Nutrition
   d) Disease
   e) Sanitation
   f) Antibiotics

**TASK 3**  *Defining complex concepts*

Many concepts and ideas are much harder to define than the ones we've looked at so far. For example, can you define **health** using the formal definition structure above?

*Health is* …………………………………………………………

If you are working in a group, share your own attempt at a definition with those of some classmates. You may find that by combining several of your definitions you will arrive at a longer but better one.

**TASK 4**  *Extracting a definition from text*

Read the text below and, with a partner, use the information in it to write a definition of **memory**.

The findings of several studies presented at this week's annual meeting of the British Psychological Society in Blackpool suggest that a shot of glucose, ginseng or Spanish sage can boost a person's memory and help them retain information.

One study, conducted at Lancaster University and the University of Western Australia, involved 60 healthy volunteers who had drinks containing either glucose or a *placebo*. They were shown a list of 20 words, which they were asked to recall half an hour later and again the next day. Researchers found that volunteers given glucose had the best memory performance – they could remember 15 words compared to 10 in the control group.

**TASK 5** *Writing a definition*

Did you need to look up a definition of *placebo* (in Task 4)? Do you understand the meaning of the word? Write a definition of *placebo*.

## The language of definition

**TASK 6** *Using clauses to structure definitions*

1  Study Table 4.1, which gives a typical structure for giving formal definitions. Then use it to answer the questions that follow.

*Table 4.1: Typical structure for formal definitions*

| Item to be defined | Verb forms<br>The Present Simple<br>(Active and Passive) | defining information |
|---|---|---|
| Good health | is …<br>means …<br>describes …<br>may be defined as …<br>can be defined as …<br>is defined as … | a state of complete physical, mental and social well-being |

a)  Complete this definition:
   A *chronic disease* ............... ...............

b)  Think of three everyday items. For each item, write a definition using one of the options in Table 4.1. If you are working with another student, test your definitions by covering the item word and seeing whether they know what you have defined.

### Clauses

There are two types of relative clause: restrictive and non-restrictive.

**A**  A person *who looks after people's teeth* is called a dentist.

**B**  Dentists, *who look after people's teeth*, are key members of the medical community.

In **A**, the relative clause is **restrictive** and tells us *what kind of* people are called dentists – 'a person who looks after people's teeth'. In **B**, the relative clause is **non-restrictive**; it allows for extra information – such as how dentists fit into the medical community – as well as telling us that they 'look after people's teeth'.

Since definitions try to narrow the meaning of an item, restrictive relative clauses are used in formal definitions. Non-restrictive relative clauses provide extra information about the subject of the main clause and can be used to expand definitions, that is, they tell us more about the item. Here is another paired example (where **C** is restrictive and **D** is non-restrictive).

  **C** Endocrine glands are *glands which secrete into the blood.*
  **D** Endocrine glands, *which secrete into the blood*, are found in various parts of the body.

**TASK 7** *Using restrictive and non-restrictive clauses*
1 Write a sentence with a restrictive clause and a sentence with a non-restrictive clause defining each of the concepts/terms below.
  a) Hypochondria
  b) Energy
  c) The World Health Organization
  d) Acupuncture
  e) Vision

### Reduced relative clauses
In academic writing, it is common to use reduced relative clauses. Sentence **E** is an example of a relative clause; whereas **F** is a reduced relative clause.

  **E** A dentist *is a person who is qualified to treat people's teeth.*
  **F** A dentist *is a person qualified to treat people's teeth.*

Sentence **F** is just as clear as **E** and it is shorter, more economical with words. Consider the following paired example.

  **G** Medicine *is a branch of science which studies and treats illness.*
  **H** Medicine *is the study and treatment of illness.*

**TASK 8** *Writing reduced relative clauses*
Reduce each of the definitions below without losing clarity.
1 A **scar** is a mark left on the skin by injury that spoils its appearance.
2 **Hair**, a dense growth of fibrous substances on certain parts of the body, helps to prevent heat loss.

3 **Smell** is the sensation that results when olfactory receptors in the nose are stimulated by particular chemicals in gaseous form in the surrounding atmosphere.

4 **Genes**, which are segments of DNA involved in producing polypeptide chains, are considered key units of heredity.

5 A **calorie** is the amount of energy, or heat, that it takes to raise the temperature of 1 gram of water 1 degree Celsius (1.8 degrees Fahrenheit). One calorie is equal to 4.184 joules, a common unit of energy used in the physical sciences.

[Definitions are adapted from http://www.cogsci.princeton.edu, extracted 17/7/04.]

## Extended definitions

An extended definition is longer than a short formal definition and it provides a fuller explanation of the concept. It might describe the concept from different perspectives: historical, political, sociological, geographical or scientific perspectives.

**TASK 9** *Using different perspectives in extended definitions*
The following text looks at health from different perspectives. Read the text and compare and contrast the WHO definition with the biomedical and the Ayurveda and Chinese definitions of good health.

## What can we learn about our health from ancient perspectives?

By Craig Hassel and Christopher Hafner

Many of us are willing to change our diets, try new products and exercise more to achieve better health. But just what do we mean by the term "health?" Defining health may not be as simple as it first appears, perhaps because health is more than just a physical condition.

The World Health Organization defines health as "a state of complete physical, mental and social well-being, and not merely the absence of disease or infirmity." Thus, a complete understanding of health encompasses all aspects of a person's well-being, including his or her mental, social, and even spiritual condition. When approached from this point of view, many factors might contribute to a person's overall health, including time of day, month or year; one's location or sense of place; presence of friends and family and a sense of community.

The culture we live in not only has a direct influence on our health, but also influences our ideas of what we mean by this term. Because most of us were educated in the United States, we tend to defer to views of health as seen from our culture and its system of health care. We have come to depend on biomedical science to explain many things about nature, including issues related to health. Consider that our modern health care system involves training physicians (including psychiatrists) to identify disease or pathology and then to formulate an appropriate treatment.

In other words, the primary focus of biomedical health care is to treat disease. Only recently has health care begun to embrace the idea of disease prevention as opposed to treatment. But the focus is still on avoiding disease, rather than enhancing well-being. Consequently, the definition of health in Western societies tends to be based on the absence or presence of disease. According to this perspective we could say one is in "good health" if one is free of any disease or symptoms that can be identified by the trained biomedical physician.

Over time, more and more people have found this definition of good health to be inadequate. This is because many people can sense changes in their well-being in the absence of disease or symptoms as defined by biomedical science. To expand our ideas of health and well-being, we may look at health from other worldviews and the ideas of health care systems that arise from these diverse worldviews.

Some societies have employed ancient systems of medicine with fundamentally different perspectives of health and nutrition. For example, Ayurveda is a way of life in India and has been practiced for more than 4,000 years. Chinese medicine is a system of health care dating back some 2,500 years. Both Ayurveda and Chinese medicine recognize well-being as something unique for each individual, and may be able to detect subtle states of imbalance within the individual well before these imbalances manifest themselves as clinically measurable indicators of disease.

[Extracted from http://www.extension.umn.edu/extensionnews/2002/LearnAboutOurHealth.html on 11/02/03]

## The place of definition in academic text

**TASK 10** *Compare and contrast definitions*

If you are working with others, choose a partner or form a small group to search the Internet for information on differences between chronic and acute diseases. You will need to find information that you can compare and contrast in order to help readers to understand the differences. Take notes as you find relevant information. Cluster the information to create two categories. List it in columns as shown on the next page.

| Chronic diseases | Acute diseases |
|---|---|
| _____ | _____ |
| _____ | _____ |
| _____ | _____ |

Definitions are used to explain the words and concepts we need, so they tend to form only part of a text and not the whole of it. We find definitions inside serious, formal writing, usually when something is being introduced for the first time. As well as using definitions to clarify the meaning of new, more specific words in a text, we can also use definitions to clarify more abstract ideas, such as issues and areas of intellectual disagreement.

**TASK 11** *Writing definitions of more abstract ideas*

The text *Measuring Children's Dental Health* includes a number of definitions. Read it and then:

1 Write a comprehensive definition of good dental health for children.
2 Explain why periodontal (gum) disease is not included in most definitions of good dental health.

# Measuring Children's Dental Health

Good dental health is usually defined as the absence of dental caries (tooth decay) and gingivitis (gum disease), combined with proper tooth and jaw function. Teeth that have never experienced any decay are considered the healthiest, and teeth in which decay has been treated (that is, the cavities have been filled) are considered healthier than teeth with untreated decay. The most comprehensive definition of good dental health would also include the appearance of the teeth: poorly aligned, crowded, mottled, or yellowed teeth are considered inferior, although their inferiority may be purely aesthetic.

The most frequently used indicators of dental health, both in individual children and in populations of children, are based on the presence of treated and untreated tooth decay. Other elements of children's dental health, such as proper tooth alignment and appearance, had not been captured in an index suitable for population studies until very recently, and are rarely collected as part of large-scale surveys in the United States. Periodontal (gum) disease is most prevalent in adults over 35, and is a significant factor contributing to tooth loss for older adults, but because the most severe forms of periodontal disease are found only infrequently in children, the presence of periodontal disease is rarely used as a measure of dental health in children.

[Extracted from http://www.futureofchildren.org/information2827 on 12/02/03]

**TASK 12** *Writing an extended definition*

Write an **extended definition** of a concept/term from your own field of studies. In your definition, you should discuss how the definition of this term has changed over time.

You should use sources (such as books and articles) from your field to help you with the content, but you should write the definition in your own words. Make your definition about 100 words or longer.

## The writing process: Understanding academic vocabulary

Pre-writing is the name given to a wide variety of techniques that help writers develop ideas and process information before writing their own text. These techniques are especially useful to new academic writers in helping them to understand and learn to *use* special vocabulary for a subject area. ***Reading*** is a good pre-writing activity – it is particularly useful in helping you to understand the vocabulary of the chosen area. Record those terms likely to be of particular use as you read.

**TASK 13** *Establishing meaning then writing a definition*

If you are working with others, form a pair or small group and find out the meaning of the word ***stress***. Together write a clear definition of it – either a brief definition (a sentence or two) or an extended definition (roughly a paragraph). Then do some reading or discussion with others to find out some of the kinds of stress that exist.

**TASK 14** *Finding relevant information and clustering it*

1 Read the text on the next page which focuses on one kind of stress: test anxiety. Then visit the website where this text was retrieved. (Note: websites go out of date. You can find other sites on the same topic by using a search engine such as www.google.com or www.askjeeves.com.)

# Do you suffer from test anxiety?

If you do, or have someone close to you who does, then you know that it really is suffering. A little nervousness before an exam can sharpen a person's attention and help him or her to do better, but tension that is persistent and extreme can prove disastrous.

"It's all in your head."

Extreme anxiety is a problem that comes from the mind trying to be helpful – maybe a little too helpful. When a person perceives some possible threat to himself or herself (physically, emotionally or socially) a part of the brain signals for changes to occur. The heart rate increases, stress hormones are released into the blood stream and blood flow is decreased to the brain and digestive system and increased to the muscles. This is fine if the person is in physical danger and needs only to react, but it is not helpful when one needs to think.

To top it all off, the stress hormones that are released into the blood stream **can negatively affect a person's memory.** When scientists gave volunteers a stress hormone (cortisol) they found that memory and thinking ability declined with an increase of the hormone. The longer they were given the hormone, the greater the impact (*Archives of General Psychiatry*, June 1999). When the hormone got out of the system – the memory and thinking ability returned. That helps to explain the reason a person will know material before and after a test but have difficulty remembering while he or she is taking the exam.

[Extracted from http://www.thestressoflife.com/test_stress.htm retrieved 12/7/04]

2 With one or more partners, access other information about solutions for test anxiety. Make notes of the information and ideas as you collect it. It is a good idea to *cluster* the information by writing it on a page (paper or screen) so that you can pre-organise the material you are going to use – in preparation for writing about solutions to test anxiety.

Look at the clustering you have done. Consider whether you have used what you learned in Units 2 and 3 about classes and categories, and about making comparisons and contrasts, to help you build sensible clusters to identify/classify defining features. Make any necessary changes to make your pre-writing more useful for writing a text.

**TASK 15** *Writing a text following on from a definition*

Test anxiety is a problem for many students; you have been finding solutions. Put your pre-writing into an organised text of approximately 500 words that contains a definition of test anxiety and explains why it is a problem; goes on to describe the solutions that have been recommended; and includes suggestions of your own, if you have any.

# Generalisations, facts and academic honesty

## UNIT 5

This unit aims to improve your writing skills by:

1. introducing the Honesty Principle
2. providing practice in writing generalisations that reflect the evidence
3. showing how to use generalisations as a basis for organising your writing
4. showing how to work with a peer group to prepare a literature review.

## The Honesty Principle

The **Honesty Principle** says *only say (or write) that for which you have evidence.* This is an important principle for academic writers because there are many people who will read academic work closely, and criticise any generalisations or claims that are not supported by evidence. Following the Honesty Principle helps you to write carefully considered statements and avoid exaggerated generalisations.

**Generalisations** are very important in academic writing. The sentence you have just read is a generalisation and exemplifies one important function of generalisations: they are very useful for starting off a piece of writing or a paragraph. They allow the writer to introduce the main properties of a concept in one statement – the generalisation – the details of which can then be developed in the text using appropriate information structures, such as examples, classifications and definitions.

**TASK 1** *Recognising the role of generalisations in texts*

Texts **A** to **D** start with a generalisation. Read each text, then write out the generalisation and say what follows: a comparison, an example, a classification or a definition (or more than one of these).

---

**Text A**

### UK Demographic Trends

The latest Government Social Trends reports show that more women are having babies in their early 30s than in their early 20s. There were 87 births per 1000 women aged 30 to 34 in 1993 compared with only 82 per 1000 among 20 to 24 year-olds in the same year.

[Extracted from http://www.on-the-net.com/interskills/minis/popul.htm on 13/02/03]

---

Answer: ................................................................................................................

## Text B

## World Over-Population and Its Effect

In 1995, UN figures suggested that the world population was expected to grow to 6 billion by 1996/8, 7 billion by 2005 and 8 billion by 2015. World population growth can be roughly classified into four main categories of percentage rates of growth on the evidence of the fertility of parents in the 1900–1994 period. These are as follows: (a) 0 to 0.79 per cent growth (UK and Ireland, Europe, Former Soviet Union); (b) 0.8 to 1.59 per cent growth (US, Canada, Caribbean, Australia and New Zealand, China and Eastern Asia); (c) 1.6 to 2.39 per cent (Central America, South America, India and Southern Asia, South-eastern Asia); (d) 2.4 per cent + (Middle East, Western Asia, Africa).

[Extracted from http://www.on-the-net.com/interskills/minis/popul.htm on 13/02/03]

Answer: ...........................................................................................................

## Text C

## Infant Mortality in Viet Nam

Viet Nam has a fairly well-developed health care system. Although it is one of the world's poorest countries, its incidence of infant mortality is relatively low. The 1997 Viet Nam Demographic and Health Survey found that the infant mortality rate was 44 deaths per thousand live births (in the period 1989–1994), and the estimate from the 1999 census was 37 per thousand in 1999 (NCPFP, 1999). By comparison, the United Nations estimates that the infant mortality rate for countries in the world considered as the "least developed" averaged 109 deaths per thousand live births in the period 1990–1995 (United Nations, 1997).

[http://www.unescap.org/esid/psis/population/journal/2002/v17n1az.pdf retrieved 15/02/03]

Answer: ...........................................................................................................

## Text D

## Go for wholegrains

The consumption of refined carbohydrates such as white bread, white rice and pasta causes the body to produce insulin and insulin-like substances that have cancer-causing potential. Wholegrains such as wholemeal bread, brown rice and wholewheat pasta limit the amount of insulin the body produces. They are also richer in fibre and nutrients, which help protect against cancer.

Dr John Briffa, So what does the doctor order? *The Observer* Sunday October 10, 2004

Answer: ...........................................................................................................

····························

: **TASK 2** *Identifying where the Honesty Principle has failed*

Look at Texts **A** to **D** again: one of them breaks the Honesty Principle because it has not produced any evidence nor has it been written in a way that avoids making too strong a generalisation. Which one is it?

····························

: **TASK 3** *Ensuring generalisations have specific support*

Look again at the three texts above that adhere to the Honesty Principle: in each of them, the generalisation is accompanied by some specific evidence which supports the generalisation.

Choose one of the three texts and find some further support for the claim made; write an additional sentence (or two) that could immediately follow the text. If you do not have good evidence for a generalisation, you will need to *hedge* – see 'The language of generalisation' later in this unit.

····························

: **TASK 4** *Recognising the interaction of generalisations and other information structures*

1 The short extract below is taken from the introduction to a research report studying the effects of marriage between close relatives ('parental consanguinity') on the offspring (children) of the marriage. It shows how a generalisation can relate to a number of other information structures. Read the extract, then do the following.

   a) State the reason for the reinvestigation of the topic (the research gap: look back at Unit 3 to remind yourself about this).
   b) Circle the definition.
   c) Underline the generalisation.
   d) Write *class* next to the classification.

## Parental Consanguinity and Offspring Mortality:
## The Search for Possible Linkage in the Indian Context

The main reason for reinvestigating the possible linkage between consanguinity and offspring mortality emerged as a result of the gross disagreement among researchers on this subject. For the purpose of this study, consanguinity is defined as marriage between relatives who share at least one common and detectable ancestor. There is no common consensus in the field of human genetics or demographic research regarding the biological impact of parental consanguinity on the health of their offspring. However, in this regard it is possible to recognize three broad schools of thought. Adherents of the first school consider that there is an overwhelming possibility of consanguineous parents having an unhealthy child.

[http://www.unescap.org/esid/psis/population/jour nal/2002/v17n1az.pdf retrieved 15/02/03]

**TASK 5** *Recognising difficulties with generalisations*

The problem with generalisations is that they can very easily lead to exaggeration – to making a claim that is greater than the facts honestly allow. An example is the text below, which was written by a student who had read text A in Task 1.

---

UK Demographic Trends

The latest Government Social Trends report very worrying changes in women's reproductive behaviour. Nowadays women are having babies in their early 30s instead of in their early 20s. Babies born to older mothers might be less healthy than babies born to younger mothers, so there are long-term implications for the health of the nation.

---

1 If you are working in a group, choose a partner and together do some text and Internet research on this topic. Then rewrite the short text above to make it reflect an ***honest*** assessment of:
   a) the **facts** of the change in maternal age at childbirth from 1990 to approximately 2000
   b) the best available **evidence** of any maternal, infant or national health implications.

## The language of generalisation

Unless there is evidence to show 100 per cent certainty, academic writers do not use absolute generalisations. They use special language to make sure that their generalisations reflect their level of certainty about a statement. *Hedges* are uses of language that let people write (or speak) in a limited way and avoid overgeneralisations. This is in line with the **Honesty Principle**.

**TASK 6** *Modifying generalisations according to the Honesty Principle*

1 Read the text on the next page and do the following.
   a) Underline the phrases which show that the writer is hedging the reasons for Germany's declining population.
   b) Explain why the writer hedges.

## Negative Growth

Germany is experiencing a period of negative growth ($-0.1\%$), which means that the population is decreasing. The German population could have shrunk due to a low birth rate and a stable death rate. Increased emigration may also be a contributing factor.

http://geography.about.com/library/weekly/aa71497.htm

2  In the following text, the writer states that there is no common agreement regarding the biological impact but then goes on to say there are three schools of thought, thus indicating that there is some agreement.
   a)  Underline the phrases the writer uses to hedge the apparent contradiction.
   b)  Explain why the writer hedges.

There is no common consensus in the field of human genetics or demographic research regarding the biological impact of parental consanguinity on the health of their offspring. However, in this regard it is possible to recognize three broad schools of thought ...

[*Asia-Pacific Population Journal*, Vol. 17, No.1]

**TASK 7**  *Hedging generalisations*

Table 5.1 gives some guidelines on the language available to writers for hedging their degree of certainty or their degree of commitment to their statements.

1  Study the table on the next page and insert the following items into the numbered gaps.

| | | |
|---|---|---|
| many | always | certainly |
| scarcely ever | improbable | is |
| possible | could/could not | |

Table 5.1 Examples of language for hedging generalisations

| Degree of certainty | Quantity | Frequency | Adjectives | Adverbs | Verbs |
|---|---|---|---|---|---|
| Complete | all/every/ each<br>no/none/<br>not any | ... (1) ...<br><br>never | definite<br>certain<br>undoubted<br>clear | ... (2) ...<br>definitely<br>undoubtedly<br>clearly | will/will not<br>... (3) ... /are (not)<br>must<br>have to |
| *high* | a majority (of)<br><br>... (4) ... /much<br><br><br><br>some/several | usual(ly)<br>normal(ly)<br>general(ly)<br>as a rule<br>on the whole<br>often | probable<br>likely | presumably<br>probably/<br>probable<br>likely | should<br>would<br>ought to |
| Partial | a number of | frequent(ly) | | ... (5) ...<br>possibly | can/cannot<br>... (6) ... |
| | | sometimes<br>occasional(ly) | uncertain | perhaps<br>maybe | may/may not<br>might/might not |
| | a minority<br>a few/a little<br>few/little | | | | |
| *low* | | rare(ly)<br>seldom<br>hardly ever<br>... (7) ... | unlikely<br>... (8) ... | | |
| Impersonal (i.e. no commitment from writer) | There is evidence to suggest that …<br>It is said that …<br>X reports that … | | | | |

........................

**TASK 8**  *Verbs used in 'hedging'*

There is also a group of verbs that can be used to refer to acts such as forecasting, suggesting and proposing. Often these verbs perform a **hedging** function in an academic text because all those acts are non-factual. Some useful verbs from this class are:

> to seem, to appear, to believe, to assume, to suggest, to speculate, to estimate, to tend, to think, to argue, to indicate, to project, to forecast

Use the above verbs to make statements 1–5 (below) more hedged. There are often many alternatives that can be used, so list all the verbs that fit the purpose.

1 Scientists <u>say</u> that the population of Europe will decline by 20% in the next fifty years.
2 The figures <u>show</u> that migration to the cities will slow down over the next twenty years.
3 When a region is hit by a food shortage, the inhabitants <u>will migrate</u>.
4 Two-thirds of the world's population <u>live</u> in poverty and misery.
5 There <u>are</u> three broad schools of thought regarding overpopulation.

**TASK 9** *Boosting generalisations*

So far we have looked at language resources for downplaying claims – for when the evidence is not total. But there are also times when a writer needs to **boost** or **strengthen** a generalisation, because she or he believes it strongly or finds it extremely important.

1 Explain to your partner the difference between these two sentences:
   a) Researchers are divided over the claim.
   b) Researchers are deeply divided over the claim.
2 Which of the following sentences have been boosted? Can you suggest why these writers wanted to strengthen the generalisations?
   a) What is vitally important here is the methodology.
   b) Some researchers have suggested that student writers may need long-term practice in grammar.
   c) Research has clearly indicated that students want feedback on their grammar errors.

**TASK 10** *Language for boosting generalisations*

Boosters have a heightening effect on generalisations. Study the sentences below and complete the sentences using the underlined words in Table 5.2

● Scientists …(1)… disagree about the causes of AIDS.
● Medical science is …(2)… opposed to the vitamin supplement industry.
● The statement issued by the research team is …(3)… suspect in these circumstances.
● There is a …(4)… division between the two sections of the research community.
● The research is a very …(5)… investigation into the causes of this phenomenon.

*Table 5.2 Examples of language for boosting generalisations*

| Adjectives | Adverbs |
|---|---|
| complete | completely |
| (very) full | fully |
| (very) thorough | thoroughly |
| total | totally |
| extreme | entirely |
| absolute | absolutely |
| definite | definitely |
| great | greatly |
| deep | deeply |
| strong | strongly |
| high | highly |

**TASK 11** *Adding hedges and boosters to a text*

Fill the gaps 1–6 below by inserting these missing hedges and boosters:

almost
close
is forecast
is projected
vastly
well

The decline in the number of babies per woman is the biggest story in global population. … (1) … everywhere fertility is in decline. But it is the poor who have the children.

The overall fertility rate – the number of children per woman – in high-income countries was 1.6 between 1995 and 2000. According to the United Nations Population Division, it … (2) … to fall further, but then rise towards 1.85 by 2045–2050. The US is now the only high income country with a fertility rate … (3) … to replacement, at 2.11. In developing countries fertility is still … (4) … above replacement rate at 2.92 children per woman. But this is … (5) … down from six children half a century ago. By 2030–2035, fertility … (6) …. to reach replacement levels and then drop below it.

http://www.on-the-net.com/interskills/minis/popul.htm visited 13/02/03

............................

**TASK 12** *Controlling levels of generalisations*

The following text has several boosters in it. If you are studying in a group, work with a partner or a small group to underline the boosters and then rewrite each sentence to make it a) neutral; b) hedged. Look back at Unit 3 if you need to remind yourself about making a reasonable claim.

> By the middle of the 21st century we will certainly have a detailed picture of the history of the universe. The parameters in our current cosmological models will have been measured to high precision, and we will know lots of other facts about the universe. It is unlikely that the Big Bang theory will be modified in the coming fifty years; in fact, it will be old fashioned to consider theories of the expanding universe testable by detailed observations.
>
> [Adapted from L. Smolin, *The future of the nature of the universe*, in J. Brockman (ed.) *The next fifty years* (pp. 9–11). Vintage Books, 2002.]

............................

**TASK 13** *Writing generalisations from graphs*

Graphs are very useful in academic texts; they allow the presentation of a large amount of factual information in a small space. Unit 6 in *Study Reading* helps you learn to read graphs and other visual information.

Study Graphs 1 and 2 on the next page. Graph 1 indicates actual and projected total population for the world from 1950 to 2050. Graph 2 shows the actual and projected world population *growth* rates for the same period.

1 Write generalisations for each of the following.
  a) What is the general trend for world population according to Graph 1?
  b) What is the general trend for world population growth rate according to Graph 2?
  c) How much of Graphs 1 and 2 are based on actual recorded data?
  d) How much of Graphs 1 and 2 are based on projected data?
2 Now write a paragraph, on the data provided in the two graphs, that makes suitably hedged generalisations. End your paragraph with a sentence that *makes a claim* about what the population of the world is likely to look like by 2100. Talk to one or more classmates or your teacher and evaluate the strength of your own claim, and then make any changes necessary for it to satisfy the Honesty Principle.

Graph 1

**World Population: 1950-2050**

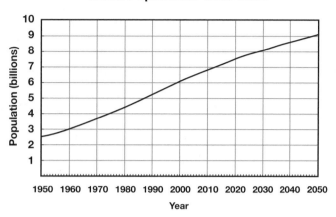

http://www.census.gov/ipc/www/world.html

Graph 2

**World Population Growth Rate: 1950-2050**

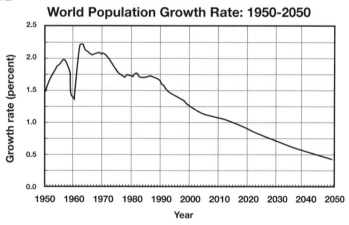

http://www.census.gov/ipc/www/world.html

# Writing a literature review

Every piece of research writing needs to review the relevant texts in its field of study, that is, to include a literature review. The purpose of a literature review is to situate your research in its context and explain its importance to your field of study. Your review should be proportional to the size of your project; the background reading for an undergraduate essay is less comprehensive than that required for a postgraduate dissertation, so the write-up of that reading into a literature review will also be shorter.

........................
:
:
**TASK 14** *Predicting information in a literature review*

You are going to read an extract from the literature review section of an article about the consequences of high-stakes tests. (High-stakes tests are tests that have a big influence on a person's future, for example, one that allows someone to 'graduate' from high school or get a university place.)

If you are interested in high-stakes tests, you can find the full article at: http://www.pop.psu.edu/general/pubs/working_ papers/psu-pri/wp0301.pdf (12-12-03). The full reference is: Reardon, S.F. and C. Galindo, *Do High-Stakes Tests Affect Students' Decisions to Drop Out of School? Evidence from NELS.* Paper prepared for presentation at the Annual Meeting of the American Educational Research Association, New Orleans, LA, April 1–5, 2002.

1 Read the first part of the literature review, below.

> Six years ago, when Reardon reviewed existing research, there was almost no empirical evidence regarding the effects of high-stakes testing on student motivation, achievement, and dropout patterns (Reardon 1996). In recent years, however, several analyses of survey data have been published. The evidence from these, however, is mixed.

2 Predict what the writers will do in the second part:
   a) describe the evidence for the reader.
   b) move on to review another area.
   c) give their opinion why the evidence is mixed.
3 Now read the second part (below) and check your prediction.

> The best quality evidence on the association between high-stakes testing and dropping out comes from two recent analyses of the relationship between high school graduation test requirements and school completion using NELS data (Jacob 2001; Warren and Edwards 2001). Although Jacob (2001) found no reading and math achievement differences associated with the presence of graduation tests, he found that dropout rates are roughly 6.5% greater among students in the bottom quintile on achievement tests in states with high school graduation test requirements than comparable students in states without such tests. Warren and Edwards (2001), however, find no effect of graduation tests on the probability of dropping out. Warren and Edwards, moreover, like Jacob, test for an interaction between the graduation test requirement and student achievement levels, in order to see if test policies disproportionately impact low-achieving students, but they find no interaction.

4 Now predict what the writers will do in the third part:
   a) move on to review another area.
   b) suggest why they found no interaction.
   c) dismiss the results as useless.
5 Read the third part (below) and check your prediction.

> The discrepancy between the Jacob (2001) and Warren and Edwards (2001) results is puzzling, since both use the same data. There are some differences in the variables included in their models, but not dramatic ones. A close examination of the precise NELS sample they use, however, reveals a potential reason for the discrepancy. Warren and Edwards use school administrator reports about the presence of a graduation test requirement as their treatment variable. Jacob points out, however, that this data is missing for a number of students (971 of 12,171 students in his sample are missing this variable). Importantly, it is missing in most of these cases because these students had dropped out of school and so had no school administrator questionnaire in their record. Warren and Edwards find no effect of the tests on dropout rates, but that may be because they have excluded from their sample a large number of dropouts, who may have disproportionately dropped out of schools with graduation test requirements.

From here the writers go on to suggest a second possible reason for the discrepancy. Notice how they claim a gap in the research.

> On balance then, neither Jacob's nor Warren and Edwards' results can be taken as definitive. It would be useful to reanalyze the NELS data using Jacob's sample and Warren and Edwards' models.

As you have seen in the example above, writing a literature review requires skills in summarising. Each research article reviewed has to be reduced to a sentence – or maybe 2–3 sentences for the most important articles you review. To do this, you need to decide what is most **relevant** to your own work from the article (or book chapter, and so on). Remember to think about your *research gap* when you are deciding what information is relevant to include in your literature review.

................

**TASK 15** *Writing a summary*
Read the text below. Summarise the difference between overcrowding and overpopulation.

Overcrowding can be eased by changing some of the variables. For example, one symptom of the disorder caused by overcrowding, traffic congestion, can be eased by building new roads. Space permitting, the area can be expanded, such as in Hong Kong, where much of the harbour has been filled in for the construction of housing, airports, hotels and roads.

Overpopulation, on the other hand, occurs when there are so many individuals in an isolated area – one in which the population must survive on their own resources – that the resources they need become used up at a rate faster than those resources can be replenished, and when the population produce waste faster than they can dispose of it.

In other words, everyone on earth could fit in the state of Texas. However, while we might all *fit* in Texas, we couldn't all *live* there without bringing in food, water and energy from elsewhere, or without exporting our bodily wastes and waste produced from households and workplaces. It would be impossible for a land surface the size of Texas to produce enough food to feed the population, especially because every square foot of useable agricultural land would already be occupied by someone's feet.

[Learn more about this at: http://www.improb.com/teach/lessons2002/people-in-texas.html retrieved 12-9-2002]

# The writing process: Working with a peer group

................

**TASK 16** *Researching ideas and information for a text*
In Task 17, you will be asked to write a 500-word literature review for the following essay topic:

Is the world overpopulated?

To prepare for this task, carry out steps 1–3.

1  If you are studying in a group, work together to consult sources both printed (such as encyclopaedias, books and articles) and electronic (such as the Internet and CDs).
      Some of your group should look up overpopulation on one of the search engines (www.lycos.com/; www.google.com/; www.yahoo.com/; or one of many others). The remainder of the group should concentrate on printed resources.
2  Then meet with the group and **brainstorm** a list of topics that have come to your attention from printed and Internet sources in the broad area of overpopulation/population.
3  With the group, **organise** the ideas you have all brainstormed by clustering (mind mapping).

## Brainstorming and clustering

Clustering is valuable for understanding the relationships between the parts of a broad topic and for developing sub-topics. Here's a useful way of doing it.

**Step 1**  Write down your topic in the middle of a blank piece of paper and circle it (in this task, the topic is *overpopulation*).

**Step 2**  In a ring around the topic circle, write down what you see as the main parts of the topic; draw a smaller circle around each one.

**Step 3**  In a ring around each main part circle, write down examples, facts or details as you find them out. Each main part, together with the ring of ideas around it, form the **clusters**.

**Step 4**  As one idea leads to another, you will draw lines to show the connections.

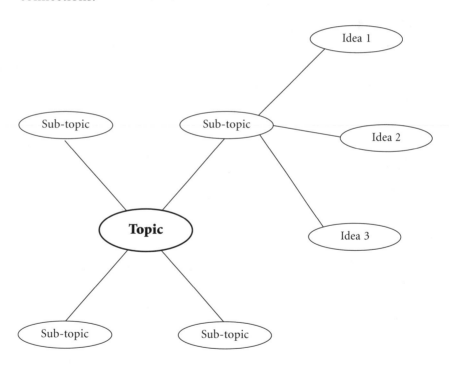

**Step 5**  Clustering should enable you to tell if you need to do more research on your topic. When you think you've finished, look at the paper you've worked on, or at the computer screen, as a whole: check that each cluster really does represent a clear area that is in some way(s) different from the other areas relating to the main topic. You might need to make a few adjustments. You can use your clustered thinking to organise how your peer group will work on Task 17.

**TASK 17** *Writing a summary based on clustering*

To complete this task, carry out steps 1–5.

1 The group can **divide the work** of further research into each aspect of this topic by taking one cluster each and carefully reading some of the source material you came across during your web and library search.

2 Read *only* enough to **clarify** why each sub-topic or issue is important: knowing too much about the topic is going to get in your way when writing a summary.

3 By e-mail, or discussion after class, together work out which material seems most important and, therefore, how much each of you should write and in what order. Then **write your own piece** of the summary and send it to everybody. Make sure you set a deadline – and that everyone knows they are responsible for keeping to that deadline.

4 You now need to **integrate the different parts**. Assign a group member to be Editor. The Editor pastes all the parts of the summary together in order and sends it to the group members.

5 The best way to finish this task may be to meet up in front of a single computer and **decide on any changes** that need to be made.

**The final version of the paper will be evaluated by your teacher.**

# UNIT 6 Seeing ideas and sharing texts

This unit aims to improve writing skills by:

1. examining techniques for writing about events in time
2. practising the use of tenses to signal time and sequence relationships
3. showing how cohesion can help readers see time relationships in text
4. showing how to 'read' the visuals (illustrations) within texts
5. showing how to write about visuals
6. giving guidance on how to give, and receive, formal peer feedback.

## Writing about events in time

In many kinds of writing, an organisational pattern is used that is based on a sequence of events: most stories and novels are like this. This is called **narrative**. A narrative usually starts with the earliest time and proceeds to the latest time.

Narrative organisation is also used in academic writing. Typical tenses used for this are: Simple Past Active (Mammals first *appeared* in …), Simple Past Passive (*It was discovered* that …) and the Past Perfect Active (He *had* always *been interested* in … ); future time is often important too.

**TASK 1** *Understanding the order of events*

Languages develop and change over time. With another student, read the text below and fill in the chart on the next page with the *chronology* of the text. If you do not know what *chronology* means, look it up in a dictionary or on the web.

## The Early Period

Before the Anglo-Saxon invasions, the language (or languages) spoken by the native inhabitants of the British Isles belonged to the Celtic family, introduced by a people who had come to the islands around the middle of the first millennium BC. Many of these settlers were, in turn, eventually subjugated by the Romans, who arrived in 43 BC. But by 410 the Roman armies had gone, withdrawn to help defend their Empire in Europe. After a millennium of settlement by speakers of Celtic, and half a millennium by speakers of Latin, what effect did this have on the language spoken by the arriving Anglo-Saxons?

[Extracted from David Crystal *The Cambridge Encyclopaedia of the English Language*, Cambridge University Press.]

```
┌─────────────────────────────────────────────────────────────────┐
│                                                                   │
└─────────────────────────────────────────────────────────────────┘

┌─────────────────────────────────────────────────────────────────┐
│                                                                   │
└─────────────────────────────────────────────────────────────────┘

┌─────────────────────────────────────────────────────────────────┐
│                                                                   │
└─────────────────────────────────────────────────────────────────┘

┌─────────────────────────────────────────────────────────────────┐
│                                                                   │
└─────────────────────────────────────────────────────────────────┘
```

**TASK 2** *Making your own chronology*

With another student, read the text below and make your own chart showing its chronology. You should have at least five stages.

> After the Angles, Saxons and Jutes invaded England, the islands of Britain were divided into many tribes and nations, and in the next four centuries languages were part of the battleground. In the fifth to eighth centuries, four main spoken dialects of English developed:
> **Northumbrian** in Northumbria
> **Mercian** in the Kingdom of Mercia
> **West Saxon** in the Kingdom of Wessex
> **Kentish** in Kent.
>
> During the 7th and 8th Centuries, Northumbria's culture and language dominated Britain. The Viking invasions of the 9th Century brought this domination to an end (along with the destruction of Mercia). Only Wessex remained as an independent kingdom. By the 10th Century, the West Saxon dialect became the official language of Britain. Written **Old English** is mainly known from this period. It was written in an alphabet called *Runic*, derived from the Scandinavian languages. The *Latin* Alphabet was brought over from Ireland by Christian missionaries and has remained the writing system of English.
>
> [Extracted from David Crystal *The Cambridge Encyclopaedia of the English Language*, Cambridge University Press.]

*Time expressions*

You will have noticed that in English, as in all languages, certain expressions help you follow the time relationships between events. In academic writing, time usually follows our experience of time in everyday life, that is, moving forward from an earlier point to a later time. As a result, the most common tense used is the Past Simple Active. But we can also manipulate time in our writing, using time expressions to move forward or backwards in time according to our purpose in writing. This is similar to the flashback and flash-forward sequences we are familiar with in the cinema.

Table 6.1 lists some common time expressions which either mark a specific time **A** or show the relationship between times **B**. You will find more of these as your academic reading and writing develop.

*Table 6.1 Some common time expressions*

| A **Time Indicators** | then, just then, at that time, in those days, last Friday, next year, at the beginning of June, five years ago, in (+ date), (etc.) |
|---|---|
| B **Time Relaters** Time before | until (then), by (then), before (then), up to that time, in the weeks/months/years leading up to, prior to, (etc.) |
| At the same time as | in the meantime, at that very moment, during, simultaneously, (etc.) |
| Time after | subsequently, after, afterwards, then, next, presently, after a while, later (on), in due course, eventually, finally, at last, (etc.) |

## TASK 3 *Using time expressions*

The time expressions have been removed from the short text below. Use the list above to help you fill in all the blanks with suitable time expressions.

…(1)…, the vocabulary of Old English consisted of an Anglo-Saxon base with borrowed words from the Scandinavian languages (Danish and Norse) and Latin.

…(2)… 1066 the Normans conquered Britain. French …(3)… became the language of the Norman aristocracy and added more vocabulary to English.

It wasn't …(4)… the 14th Century that English became dominant in Britain again. …(5)… 1399, King Henry IV became the first king of England …(6)… the Norman Conquest whose mother tongue was English. …(7)… the 14th Century, the dialect of London had emerged as the standard dialect of what we …(8)… know as Middle

English. The Middle English period lasted from the 14th ...(9)... the 16th centuries.

...(10)... the 16th Century, because of the contact that the British have had with many peoples from around the world, many words have entered the language. Also, ...(11)... the Renaissance of classical learning, new words were created at an increasing rate. ...(12)... Shakespeare coined over 1600 words. This process is ...(13)... happening in the modern era.

[Adapted from: *The Cambridge Encyclopaedia of the English Language*]

## TASK 4 *Recognising the timing of events*

In academic writing, writers do not always write things in the order in which they happened. They change the order for emphasis or to clarify important relationships. They use **verb tenses** to signal the order in which things happened.

All the verbs in the text below have been numbered. Decide whether the verbs refer to the Present, Past or Future. The first three are done for you.

| 1 Present | 2 Future | 3 Past | 4 | 5 |
|-----------|----------|--------|----|----|
| 6 | 7 | 8 | 9 | 10 |
| 11 | 12 | 13 | 14 | 15 |
| 16 | 17 | 18 | 19 | 20 |
| 21 | 22 | 23 | | |

### Gondwanaland

Our planet (1) is still changing and (2) will continue to do so. 'Gondwanaland' (named after an aboriginal tribe in India, the Gonds) is a proposed ancient super-continent that (3) was comprised of the land masses that we now (4) know as South America, India, Australia, Africa, and Antarctica.

The breaking up of Gondwanaland, the dispersion of the various continental landmasses, the drifting of the Antarctic continent towards the South Pole and its isolation, (5) are all relatively recent events by the scale of geological time.

Geological and fossil evidence (6) suggest that

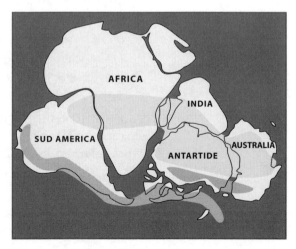

Diagram A

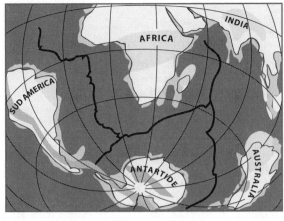

Diagram B

until the Jurassic Age 140 million years ago, the supercontinent of Gondwanaland, (7) included Antarctica, Africa, Arabia, India, Ceylon, Australia, New Zealand and South America, and (8) occupied temperate latitudes (see Diagram A). As Diagram B (9) shows, eighty million years ago, the land which (10) was to become Aotearoa (later (11) called New Zealand by white settlers), (12) broke free from Gondwanaland and (13) set off on a life of peculiar isolation during which it (14) had no association with any other landmass, the longest geological and ecological isolation of any land on Earth. Mammals (15) hadn't arrived in Gondwanaland at the time of the split, and nor (16) had snakes, and Aotearoa/New Zealand (17) developed an

amazing ecology of its own. Its ecological niches (18) became filled with birds, an amazing variety of lizards and lizard-like creatures, and some rather spectacular insects.

Then, about 2000 years ago, the waka (canoes) of the Polynesian peoples (19) arrived, (20) brought with them the Polynesian rat (known in Maori as Kiore), and the decline of the indigenous biodiversity (21) started. The Europeans (22) brought many new predators, and as a result the unique ecology of New Zealand (23) is now largely gone.

[Diagrams from http://www.pnra.it/ANTARTIDE/HTML]

---

....................
:  : **TASK 5** *Explaining writer's choices*
        Why did the writer move from *present* to *future* to *past* and back to
        the *present* again in the first paragraph? Why not just start with
        Gondwanaland and continue to the present?

....................
:  : **TASK 6** *Choosing tenses*
        Verbs help to show the relationship between sentences in a text.
        In the text below, some verbs have been replaced with three choices
        (in *italics*). In each case, underline the verb form that best clarifies
        the relationship between the sentences. Notice that the three verbs in
        the first sentence (underlined) are in the Present Simple Tense (two)
        and the Present Perfect (one).

> Recent estimates place current global forest cover at about 50% of
> its original extent, and conclude that a large proportion of this loss
> has occurred within the past 50 years. Despite conservation efforts,
> many remaining forest ecosystems *were/have been/had been*

seriously degraded and fragmented, resulting in environmentally, economically and aesthetically impoverished landscapes. Loss of forest cover not only *limited/limits/is limiting* the scope of biodiversity conservation but also *diminished/diminishes/is diminishing* the prospect for attaining secure livelihoods among many rural populations throughout the developing world.

Forest restoration was *identified/has been identified/had been identified* in several contexts as a key activity for reversing the trend of forest loss and improving biodiversity conservation, ecosystem functions and improved livelihood security.

[Extracted from http://www.unep-wcmc.org/forest/restoration/index.htm]

## Connecting events in a text

**TASK 7** *Linking strategies*

There are a number of strategies that writers use to link sentences together to form texts. In boxes 1 to 7, there are a number of these strategies. Match them to the sentence examples given in boxes a) to g).

| | |
|---|---|
| 1 Repeating a word or words from the first sentence in the second sentence | a) The maize plant faces two main pests. The first is the weevil borer whose larvae eat their way through the maize plant. |
| 2 Use a synonym (word with same meaning) of a word from the first sentence in the second | b) The surroundings in which we carry out our daily lives are very important to us. We are continually aware of our environment as we go about our business. |
| 3 Use a pro-form (e.g. pronoun) in the second sentence | c) Energy in food is measured in calories. Approximately 50% of the calories we consume are used in physical activity. |
| 4 Use a sequence marker [e.g. Firstly, secondly/a), b), c)] | d) We need to make our buildings more energy efficient. We need to make our cars less polluting. |
| 5 Repeat a sentence structure | e) We are losing rain forests at a great rate. Millions of trees are being cut down every week. |
| 6 Use connectives (e.g. addition, time relaters) | f) Trees are an essential part of a city's development. They help reduce pollution and provide shade. |
| 7 Use a hyponym (e.g. police station → building/car → means of transport) | g) The UAE is spending a lot of money to improve its environment. For example it invested millions of dollars developing forests in the desert. |

**TASK 8** *Linking pro-forms*

1 Complete this text by reinserting these pro-forms:

*this* (×2)  *they* (×2)  *it* (×3)  *these  one  its  ours  we*

---

Tropical forest is being destroyed at the rate of 40,000 square miles = an area the size of Ohio, per year. ...(1)... is mainly due to slash-and-burn agriculture in areas of high population growth, in which small areas are cleared and used for a few years until ...(2)... become infertile, and then more acreage is cleared. About 44% of the original tropical forest on the earth is now gone. ...(3)... has been estimated that 15–20% of all species will become extinct by the year 2000 because of the destruction of tropical forests. ...(4)... rate is about 10,000 times as high as the rate prior to the existence of human beings.

The fundamental reason for the degradation and loss of habitat is the explosive growth of the human population. Since 1900 ...(5)... has more than tripled. Since 1950 ...(6)... has more than doubled, to 6 billion. Every year 90 million more people (= 3x the population of California) are added to the planet. All of ...(7)... people need places to live, work and play, and ...(8)... all contribute to habitat loss and global pollution.

Our generation is the first ...(9)... to really become aware of the fact that the human population is causing irreparable damage to the planet – to the air, water and soil of the planet and to ...(10)... biological resources. ...(11)... is not the first generation to do damage to the planet, but ...(12)... are the first to realize the extent of the problem.

[From: Biodiversity and Conservation: A Hypertext Book by Peter J. Bryant
http://darwin.bio.uci.edu/~sustain/bio65/lec01/b65lec01.htm]

---

2 Circle examples of repetition (for example, when a word or words from one sentence appear in the sentence that follows it) in the text above.

**TASK 9** *Using linking for cohesion*

Rewrite the following paragraphs to make them more cohesive and shorter.

Americans use more than one billion pounds of pesticides annually. They use the pesticides to combat pests on agricultural crops, in homes, business, schools, parks, hospitals, and other public places. The health effects of pesticide exposure range from mild to severe. The health effects may include: dizziness, nausea, acute poisoning, cancer, neurological effects, and reproductive and developmental harm. In many cases, the health effects are not immediate. The health effects may show up years later as unexplained illness.

The number of cases of pesticide exposure in the U.S. is alarming. The number in 1997 was 88,255 pesticide exposure emergencies. The pesticide emergencies were reported to the national network of Poison Control Centers. Fourteen fatalities were attributed to pesticide poisoning during the same period. Over 50 per cent of all reported pesticide poisoning cases involve children under six years of age. A 1998 study showed that children exposed to pesticides often have impaired hand-eye coordination. They have decreased stamina and memory impairment. They showed difficulty when asked to draw a simple picture of a person. They showed this difficulty when compared with an unexposed peer.

[Adapted from a text on http://environment.about.com/cs/pesticides/a/pesthealth.htm retrieved 1/10/04]

## Reading and writing about visuals

Diagrams, photos, charts, tables: all these and other kinds of visuals (illustrations) that are found in academic texts are there to help readers understand the message of the text. But unless you understand how to 'read' visuals they may be less helpful than they should be. We recommend that you study this aspect of reading in the *Study Reading* course book (Unit 6).

**TASK 10** *'Reading' a visual*

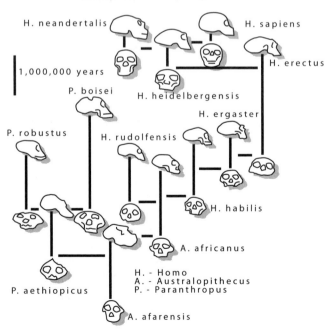

H. neandertalis

H. sapiens

1,000,000 years

H. erectus

P. boisei

H. heidelbergensis

H. ergaster

P. robustus

H. rudolfensis

H. habilis

A. africanus

H. - Homo
A. - Australopithecus
P. - Paranthropus

P. aethiopicus

A. afarensis

Evolution scientists see *the human race* as a story of biodiversity leading to a succession of new species and eventually to an extremely successful one, *homo sapiens*, which has spread right across the planet. Note that, although in English most diagrams are 'read' from left to right and from top to bottom, in *Evolution* we have to read up from the bottom (from the oldest to most recent time).

[http://www.darwin.ws/contradictions/htree.jpg retrieved 1/11/04]

**TASK 11** *Writing about a visual*

Write a short account in narrative sequence that describes the development of modern man. When you 'read' the visual, pay attention to the lines *between* the skulls. As with all flow diagrams, if there is no line, there is no connection. It will help you to know that *Homo habilis* is considered a key human ancestor.

Search the web for information to help you with the detail of this narrative. An excellent website is www.handprint.com (look up the Tour of the Hominid Fossil Record [accessed 17/11/05]).

## *Language for writing about visuals*

Here are some useful expressions for writing about visuals.

**Referring to a visual**
- As shown in Table 1/Figure 20/the chart/diagram/graph
- As can be seen from the chart/the diagram/the graph/ Table 1/Figure 3
- According to Table 1/Figure 4/the graph

**Describing trends that can be seen in a visual**
- The graph shows a rise/an increase/a fall/a drop/a decline in …
- The number of species declined dramatically/sharply/ considerably/steadily/gradually/slowly over the following one hundred years.
- The area of forest remained the same/remained stable/reached a peak/remained constant until 1978.

**TASK 12** *Selecting information from a visual*

The pie chart, below, shows in general the percentages of US species that are:

- presumed/possibly extinct
- critically imperiled (in very serious danger)
- imperiled (in serious danger)
- vulnerable (could be soon in danger).

1 If we wanted to write an article showing that US species are in danger, which statistics would we highlight?

2 Which statistics would we highlight if we wanted to show that most US species are not in danger of extinction?

3 Complete the following summary.

The pie chart ...(a)... the relative condition of species in the US. ...(b)... are not in any danger of extinction, or not seen to be, while another ...(c)... are currently in no immediate danger but are thought to be facing some ...(d).... It is thought only ...(e)... per cent
of the total population may be extinct.

4 Does the above summary present an optimistic (o) or pessimistic (p) picture of the state of US species? (o)/(p)

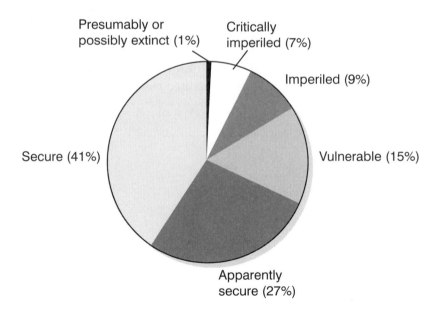

[http://www.oup-usa.org/sc/0195125193/index2.html]

··························
·
·
**TASK 13** *Extracting detail from a visual*

The bar graph below provides more specific information than that shown in the Task 12 visual. It shows the percentage of **individual** species that are:

- presumed/possibly extinct
- critically imperiled (in very serious danger)
- imperiled (serious danger)
- vulnerable (could be soon in danger).

For the purposes of this exercise, we will use three general classes to describe all the individual species: those that live on land, those that live in water, and those that can live in and out of water.

1 Of the three classes, which one is the most in danger?
2 Within the class, which individual species is most/least in danger?
3 Within the other classes, which species are most/least in danger?
4 Complete the following summary of the data.

> The data show the state of selected …(a)… relative to the four in-danger categories, vulnerable, imperiled, critically imperiled and presumed extinct. We can divide the species into …(b)… types: those that live on …(c)…, those that exist in water and those that exist on land and in …(d)…. In terms of the four in-danger categories, the water species are the focus of most concern with 69% of …(e)… in most danger followed by crayfish (51%), stoneflies (43%), freshwater fish (37%) and …(f)… (36%). Land species, on the other hand, are …(g)… imperiled with only 14% and 16% of birds and mammals in any danger, and reptiles, butterflies/Skippers, Tiger Beetles, ferns, gymnosperms and flowering plants at between 18% and …(h)….

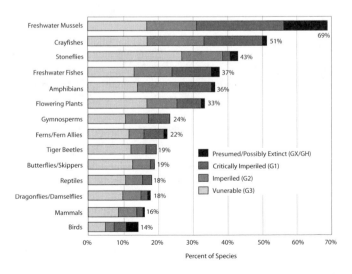

[http://www.epa.gov/bioin dicators/images/4-2sm.jpg retrieved 3/10/04]

## The writing process: Learning about peer reviews

If you have been following this part of the course you should be beginning to appreciate the ways that you and your classmates can help each other in the writing process. One of the specific ways you can give each other help is by **peer review**.

A peer review involves getting feedback on your writing from a peer (such as a classmate).

**TASK 14** *Reading-to-write about a visual*

The diagram below is an up-to-date variation on the well-known carbon cycle diagram. You are going to use the information in this visual in a complete peer feedback cycle, but first, start by making sure you understand what the visual is showing. If you need to read more about the carbon cycle and/or about the effects of deforestation, refer to encyclopaedias or visit the World Wide Web. When you feel you understand the visual properly, go on to Task 15.

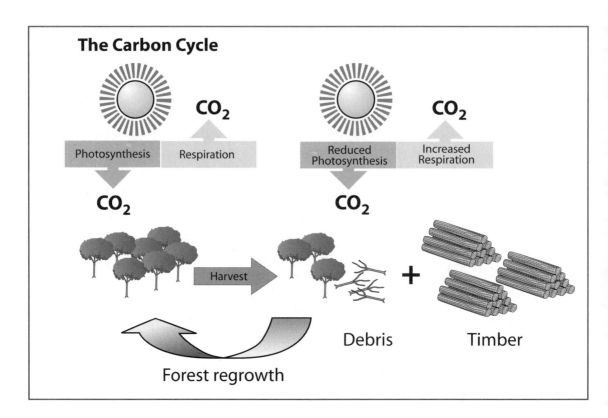

Picture from www.whrc.org: retrieved 21/8/04

**TASK 15** *Commenting on a text*

The essay below was written by a student. With some classmates, discuss what this writer could do to strengthen this writing. Remember that 'writing' includes grammar and punctuation, as well as writing style, being sensitive to readers, and being well-organised. Some aspects of the writing might be stronger (or weaker) than others.

Over half of the world's forests have been destroyed, and the current alarming rate of deforestation is seems to getting worst. Every minute an amount of land about equal to 37 football pitches gets deforested and soon we will be left with a planet empty of trees. But the world's forests are the home of many of the most important species on earth.

Forests also play a vital role in regulating the climate and making the planet habitable.

Once upon a time much of the earth was covered in trees, but the growing human population has killed most of them. This happened a long time ago in countries with mild climates like Britain and other parts of Europe because humans started growing crops several thousand years ago, and agriculture has now reduced the great European forests to tiny pockets here and there.

But the tropical forests only became threatened since the last century. There was twice as much tropical forest at the turn of the 20th century as there is today, and it is disappearing fast. In Africa about four million hectares of forest got destroyed each year, and now 45 per cent of its original forest cover has disappeared.

Deforestation is caused by commercial logging, clearance for roads and railways, forest fires, mining and drilling. Ordinary people also cut down trees for agriculture, fuelwood collection and to make space for homes, and it's hard to know who is to blame for it.

People have been living in and around tropical rainforests for tens of thousands of years. However, in the last two centuries populations have expanded, and did need more and more space for housing and agriculture and more wood for building. As richer countries have demanded more hard woods from tropical rainforests the problem has become even greater.

[From: Biodiversity and Conservation: A Hypertext Book by Peter J. Bryant http://darwin.bio.uci.edu/~sustain/bio65/lec01/b65lec01.htm]

**TASK 16** *Getting ready for peer review*

Decide on a way you'd like to continue the essay (in Task 15); you can follow any of the possible directions the writer opened up. Make sure you use some of your own previous knowledge and/or experience, and also that you do some exploration to find new information. You can work with peers as you do this, using what you learned in Unit 5 and any other peerwork suggestions your teacher has for you. **Complete the essay with at least two solid paragraphs of your own.**

Before you take part in a peer review session, follow the process below. The process here suggests using e-mail, but you can also do this on paper in the classroom.

---

1 Decide what type of feedback you want: do you need some fresh ideas? Some comments on your language? Some response on your arguments? Make notes about what you would most like your reader – your e-mail correspondent – to pay attention to as he or she reads your draft writing.

2 Turn your notes into a small number of short, clear questions you would like your partner to answer.

3 Write a short, polite e-mail message asking her or him for help.

4 Copy your list of questions into the e-mail just under your message.

---

Peer review can take place in face-to-face meetings, but it can also be done over e-mail, depending on the convenience of the people taking part. It's probably best to practise peer review face-to-face before trying it over e-mail. You will find Appendix A helpful.

**TASK 17** *Going from peer review to submitting a draft*

Think about the feedback you get from your peer. Make any changes to your writing that you think it needs. Submit the revised version to the teacher, and write a note or e-mail to the teacher explaining what peer feedback you got and how you used it.

# Description, methods and academic reality

**UNIT 7**

This unit aims to improve writing skills by:

1. looking at how to describe processes
2. introducing 'nominalisation'
3. using nominalisations in the Results section and to make texts more coherent
4. examining key aspects of the Methods section of a paper
5. practising using peer review to improve a draft of your writing.

## Describing processes and products

In Unit 6, we helped you explore the notion of time order. Here, we look at another idea closely related to time order: process order. Process order is used to describe processes, for example the life cycle of a plant; or to explain how a procedure is carried out, for example how to extract drinking water from sea water. Process order is used primarily to educate the reader. You will find it useful in your own academic writing, especially when reporting work you have done yourself.

**TASK 1** *How we write about processes*

The text on the next page describes the process of land erosion. Look at points 1–6, then carry them out by reading the text.

1 Underline the sentence that defines erosion.
2 Circle the sentence that introduces a classification.
3 How many different types of erosion are identified?
4 The text is a general description of the erosion process. What verb tense would you expect to find most often used?
5 How often are each of these tenses used? List the verbs.
   a) The Past Simple Tense
   b) The Present Simple Tense
   c) The Present Simple Passive Tense
   d) The Past Simple Passive Tense
6 Which two of these tenses are mainly used to describe erosion processes in general?
   a) The Past Simple Tense
   b) The Present Simple Tense
   c) The Present Simple Passive Tense
   d) The Past Simple Passive Tense
   e) The Present Continuous

The process of erosion occurs when the surface of the land is worn away and lost. There are many specific types of erosion. In gully erosion, thin water columns quickly remove the soil from an area. Rill erosion occurs when many tiny water channels are formed, and interrill erosion happens when a layer of soil is removed. Saltation erosion is the removal of soil and minerals by wind, water, or gravity. The soil bounces and moves away to another location. Surface creep occurs when the wind blows small particles along the ground, picking up soil particles and blowing them away through the air.

[Extracted from http://library.thinkquest.org/26026/Science/erosion.html on 09/09/2003]

## The language for writing about processes

In writing about a process we need to describe a sequence of events – the order in which they happen. This can be achieved through the use of sequence connectors, such as those in Table 7.1.

*Table 7.1: Useful sequence connectors for describing a series of events*

| Sequence connector | Purpose |
| --- | --- |
| first<br>firstly<br>first of all | Used to denote the **first** step in a process |
| second<br>secondly | Used to denote the second step in a process |
| third<br>thirdly | Used to denote the third step in a process |
| next<br>after that<br>next | Used to denote any new step in a process |
| last<br>lastly<br>final<br>finally | Used to denote the last step in a process |

**Note**: it is usual to use the set 'first, second, third … last/final' or 'firstly, secondly, thirdly … lastly/finally' rather than to mix them (for example, using 'first, secondly, third' would not be considered good English).

**TASK 2** *Using sequence connectors to describe a sequence*

1  Insert the appropriate connectors from Table 7.1 into the following text; you can also try out any other sequence words you know.

RAIN-MAKING EXPERIMENT

Here is a simple experiment that you can do in your own kitchen, and that shows how rain is formed.

...(1)... fill a glass about half full of water. ...(2)... cover the glass tightly with some plastic wrap. ...(3)... put a rubber band around the glass to hold the wrap in place. Make sure there are no holes in the wrap over the top of the glass.

...(4)... put the glass of water in the refrigerator. Wait one or two hours, or longer, and check the glass. There should be water droplets on the inside of the glass on the plastic. Water droplets on the sides of the glass show that the experiment is working. More water drops form as time goes by. ...(5)... when you see plenty of droplets, take the glass out of the refrigerator and put it in a warmer location.

...(6)... the glass begins to warm up, and the plastic will have more water than it can hold onto. ...(7)... the drops will rain back into the glass.

TASK 3 *Discovering language for writing about processes*

1 The text below describes the process of hurricane formation.
   a) Skim the text and say which verb tenses are used.
   b) Circle any phrases that are used to show the sequence/order in which events happen.

# HOW A HURRICANE FORMS

Hurricanes are fueled by water vapor that is pushed up from the warm ocean surface, so they can last longer and sometimes move much further over water than over land. The combination of heat and moisture, along with the right wind conditions, can create a new hurricane. Hurricanes form in tropical regions where the water temperature is at least 80 degrees Fahrenheit / 27 degrees Celsius, where moist air is common and winds off the equator often meet. Most Atlantic hurricanes begin off the west coast of Africa, starting as thunderstorms that move out over the warm, tropical ocean waters. As the Figure below shows, a thunderstorm reaches hurricane status in three stages. The first stage is called a 'tropical depression' and is characterized by the formation of a cluster of swirling clouds and rain with wind speeds of less than 38 mph (61.15 kph / 33 kt). The second stage is a 'tropical storm' with wind speeds of 39 to 73 mph (54.7 to 117.5 kph / 34 to 63 kt). Finally a 'hurricane' forms when wind speeds are greater than 74 mph (119 kph / 64 kt).

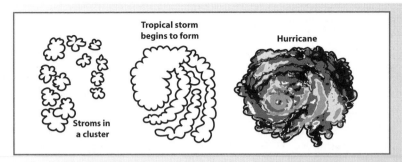

Tropical storm begins to form

Hurricane

Stroms in a cluster

It can take anywhere from hours to several days for a thunderstorm to develop into a hurricane. Although the whole process of hurricane formation is not entirely understood, three events must happen for hurricanes to form. First, there must be a continuing evaporation-condensation cycle of warm, humid ocean air. Next the patterns of wind should be characterized by converging winds at the surface and strong, uniform-speed winds at higher altitudes. The final event is that there must be a difference in air pressure (pressure gradient) between the surface and high altitude.

### Warm, Humid Ocean Air

Warm, moist air from the ocean surface begins to rise rapidly. As this warm air rises, its water vapor condenses to form storm clouds and droplets of rain. The condensation releases heat called latent heat of condensation. Then latent heat warms the cool air aloft, thereby causing it to rise. This rising air is replaced by more warm, humid air from the ocean below. This cycle continues, drawing more warm, moist air into the developing storm and continuously moving heat from the surface to the atmosphere. This exchange of heat from the surface creates a pattern of wind that circulates around a center. This circulation is similar to that of water going down a drain.

### Patterns of Wind

'Converging winds' are winds moving in different directions that run into each other. Converging winds at the surface collide and push warm, moist air upward. This rising air reinforces the air that is already rising from the surface, so the circulation and wind speeds of the storm increase. In the meantime, strong winds blowing at uniform speeds at higher altitudes (up to 30,000 ft / 9,000 m) help to remove the rising hot air from the storm's center, maintaining a continual movement of warm air from the surface and keeping the storm organized. If the high-altitude winds do not blow at the same speed at all levels – if wind shears are present – the storm loses organization and weakens.

### Pressure Gradient

High-pressure air in the upper atmosphere (above 30,000 ft / 9,000 m) over the storm's center also removes heat from the rising air, further driving the air cycle and the hurricane's growth. As high-pressure air is sucked into the low-pressure center of the storm, wind speeds increase.

[Text adapted from http://science.howstuffworks.com/hurricane2.htm visited 12/09/2003; Figure 1 Miami Museum of Science Learning Network, 2003.]

The above text uses active voice (the Present Simple) and passive voice (the Present Simple Passive). Generally speaking the active voice is clearer and usually easier to understand than the passive voice. However, there are times, particularly in scientific writing, when the passive voice is very effective. The passive is used *when the agent is obvious, unimportant or unknown.*

For example, an active sentence might read:

*Scientists call the first stage a 'tropical depression'.*

Whereas, written as a passive sentence, it would read:

*The first stage is called a 'tropical depression'.*

**Note** that the passive sentence misses out the word 'scientists' – the writer can only do this if he or she considers the agent to be 'obvious, unimportant or unknown'.

## TASK 4  *Completing a process description*

As you have seen, we often use the active voice when writing about processes because it is clear and easy to understand. The introduction to a description of tornadoes and thunderstorms (below) is a good example.

### Tornadoes and Thunderstorms

A typical thunderstorm cloud can accumulate a huge amount of energy. If the conditions are right, this energy creates a huge updraft into the cloud. But where does the energy come from?

Clouds are formed when water vapor condenses in the air.

(http://science.howstuffworks.com/tornado2.htm visited 10/09/2003)

You have also seen that the **passive** voice can be effective when it is not important **who** or **what** did something.

1  **Continue the text above** by choosing one of the three alternatives (**A**, **B** or **C**) in each row on the next page. To do this, keep in mind the different uses of active and passive verb forms, and also the need to make a complete-sounding text.

To get you started, the first answer is **1 C.**

| A | B | C |
|---|---|---|
| 1 Physical heat is released and heat is a form of energy. | Heat is a form of energy and it is released when clouds are formed. | *This change in physical state releases heat; heat being a form of energy.* |
| 2 A result of the condensation that forms the cloud is the thunderstorm's energy. | A good deal of a thunderstorm's energy is a result of the condensation that forms the cloud. | Resulting from the condensation that forms the cloud is a good deal of a thunderstorm's energy. |
| 3 About 600 calories of heat for every gram of water condensed are made available, according to *Encyclopedia Britannica*. | According to *Encyclopedia Britannica* every gram of water condensed makes available about 600 calories of heat. | According to *Encyclopedia Britannica*: for every gram of water condensed, about 600 calories of heat are made available. |
| 4 When the water freezes in the upper parts of the cloud, another 80 calories of heat per gram of water are released. | Another 80 calories of heat per gram of water are released in the upper part of the cloud. | The upper part of the cloud freezes and releases 80 calories of heat per gram of water. |
| 5 The temperature of the updraft is increased and, in part, is converted to kinetic energy. | Converted to kinetic energy, the temperature of the updraft is increased. | This energy goes to increase the temperature of the updraft and, in part, is converted to kinetic energy. |
| 6 If we know the quantity of water that is condensed in, and subsequently precipitated from a cloud, then we can calculate the total energy of a thunderstorm. | If the quantity of water that is condensed in and subsequently precipitated from a cloud is known, then the total energy of a thunderstorm can be calculated. | Then the total energy of a thunderstorm can be calculated, if the quantity of water that is condensed in and subsequently precipitated from a cloud is known. |
| 7 The energy released amounts to about 10,000,000 kilowatt-hours, which is equivalent to a 20-kiloton nuclear warhead, in an average thunderstorm. | Ten million kilowatt-hours, the energy released in an average thunderstorm is equivalent to a 20-kiloton nuclear warhead. | In an average thunderstorm, the energy released amounts to about 10,000,000 kilowatt-hours, which is equivalent to a 20-kiloton nuclear warhead. |
| 8 Ten to a hundred times more energetic might be a large, severe thunderstorm. | More energetic by 10 to 100 times is a large, severe thunderstorm. | A large, severe thunderstorm might be 10 to 100 times more energetic than the average. |

The correct answer is taken from http://science.howstuffworks.com/tornado2.htm

## Nominalisations

Academic writers frequently use the noun forms of verbs to help focus their writing on general concepts and things; rather than use verb forms which typically focus on specific actions or events. The process of turning **verbs** (actions or events) into **nouns** (things, concepts or people) is called **nominalisation**. Version 1 below shows a focus on verbs, while Version 2 focuses on nouns.

### Version 1

*In the laboratory we studied* (**action**) *how long water hyacinth can survive* (**event**) *when grown* (**event**) *in vessels filled* (**action**) *with solutions to which were added* (**action**) *different heavy metal concentrations.*

### Version 2

*A laboratory study* (**thing**) *was conducted to determine the survival* (**concept**) *of water hyacinth under several conditions of heavy metal concentrations* (**thing**).

The use of verbs in the first version emphasises actions and events; whereas the use of nominalisations in the second version emphasises concepts and things. Because of the focus on concepts, the use of nominalisations has the effect of making the writing seem more abstract and formal and hence more academic.

**TASK 5** *Using nominalisations*
Complete Version 2 using the nominalised forms of 'spreading', 'restricting' and 'flows'.

### Version 1

*Water hyacinths are rapidly spreading into drainage systems and are restricting the rate at which the water flows.*

### Version 2

*The rapid ... of water hyacinths into drainage systems is causing ... in the rate of water ... .*

**TASK 6** *Using nominalisations in a Results section*
Use these nominalisations to complete the Results section of the research paper that follows.

*distribution; earnings; employment; improvement; monitoring; production*

**An enterprise-based approach to conservation: the case of Biligiri Rangaswamy Temple wildlife sanctuary**

[A group of three community-based enterprises consisting of a honey-processing unit, a food-processing unit, and a herbal-medicine-processing unit, has been established in and near the BR (Biligiri Rangana) Hills in the Mysore district of Karnataka state, India.]

Results

- The enterprises have contributed an …(1)… in skills and capacities of community members, as the …(2)… activities in the HPU (honey-processing unit) and FPU (food-processing unit) are completely managed by the Soliga community.

- The enterprises have created direct …(3)… for the Soliga members, though on a limited scale.

- Annual …(4)… are more than Rs. 100,000 from HPU and FPU, and Rs. 30,000 from HMPU (herbal-medicine-processing unit).

- The enterprises have generated profits, and an amount of Rs. 100,000 from the accumulated profit was put aside for …(5)… to the community members in 1998.

- …(6)… for biological and socio-economic parameters have been initiated at various levels.

[http://www.teriin.org/case/biligiri.htm visited 04/10/2003]

**TASK 7** *Creating nominalisations*

Complete the table below by making nominalisations from the verbs in the left-hand column.

| Verb | Nominalisation |
|---|---|
| 1 allocate | allocation |
| 2 consume | |
| 3 create | |
| 4 develop | |
| 5 discover | |
| 6 include | |
| 7 integrate | |
| 8 select | |
| 9 separate | |
| 10 transport | |

Nominalisations can be useful in writing for three reasons.

1 The nominalisation provides a link back to a previous sentence.

   *The units can save up to 45% of the cost of fuel. Savings increase if it is used as a replacement for a petrol fuelled oven.*

2 Some nominalisations are used so much they have become like subjects.

   *Globalisation has succeeded in uniting the peoples of the world.*

3 Some sentences can be made more precise using nominalisations.

   *Another important benefit is the fact that this can be used to reduce emissions.*
   [less precise version, without nominalisation]
   *The reduction in emissions is another important benefit.*
   [more precise version, with nominalisation]

**TASK 8** *Writing sentences using nominalisations*

1 Use at least three of the verbs from Task 7 in sentences of your own.
2 Rewrite your sentences using nominalisations.
3 If you are studying in a group, exchange your nominalised sentences with a partner and see if you can replace the nominalisations in your partner's sentences with their original verbs.

**TASK 9** *Rewriting text using nominalisations*

Below is part of a text on flooding. Using nominalisations will make it seem more academic. Rewrite the underlined sections by nominalising the underlined verbs. The first one is done for you on the next page.

# Flooding

In the next section, we will see how concrete, asphalt and other things that humans (1) construct can affect flooding.

The degree of flooding is determined by how much water (2) accumulates in an area, as well as the nature of the land surface. As civilization has (3) expanded, the landscape has been changed in a number of ways. In the Western world one way in which we significantly (4) changed the landscape was by covering the ground in asphalt and concrete. Obviously, these surfaces do not (5) absorb water very well; almost all of the rain becomes runoff. In an industrialized area that is not well (6) drained, it may not take much rain to cause significant flooding.

[Adapted from: http://www.howstuffworks.com/static/flood3.htm visited14/11/04]

- In the next section, we will see how concrete, asphalt and other **human construction** can affect flooding.
- The degree of flooding is determined by the … of water in an area, as well as the nature of the land surface.
- With the … of civilization, the landscape has been changed in a number of ways.
- In the Western world, significant … were made by covering the ground in asphalt and concrete.
- Obviously, the … of these surfaces is very low: almost all of the rain becomes runoff.
- In an industrialized area that lacks good …, it may not take much rain to cause significant flooding.

## Writing the Methods section

**TASK 10** *Exploring a Methods section*

1 Read the brief extract from the Methods section of a research paper on survival of a water plant called water hyacinth below, and decide if the writers:

a) explain the general type of procedure used in the research? **Yes/No**

b) describe the variables (plants, chemicals, equipment, etc.)? **Yes/No**

c) show the procedures followed? **Yes/No**

2 Which tense(s) is/are used? List the verbs with the tense(s).

3 Does the writing provide enough information for another researcher to repeat the experiment? If you think it does not, try to find out where the gaps in the information are.

# 2 Experimental

## 2.1 Sample collection

Water hyacinth plant samples were collected from the river Nile water at Abu El Riesh village (at site, $3 \times 3$ m$^2$, approx. 1 m deep, 1.5 m from the bank), Aswan city ($24°2'$N and $32°9'$E), Egypt in September 1999 and were transferred to the laboratory in polyethylene bags. Plants of similar shape, size (weight of each plant, $200 \pm 20$ g wet mass) and height (roots, 20–22 cm; aerial parts, 26–27 cm) were selected and washed several times using tap and bidistilled water. Three of these plant samples were chosen as a blank to determine their initial metal ion concentrations before the experiments. The other plant samples were inserted in an upright position in glass boxes of $40 \times 40 \times 40$ cm$^3$

containing 30 litres of media, i.e. Nile water (from the Nile river), distilled water, wastewater (from Kima drain wastewater, Aswan, Egypt), solutions with several metals at different concentrations (1, 3, 5, 7, 10, 50 and 100 mg l$^{-1}$ of Cd, Co, Cr, Cu, Mn, Ni, Pb and Zn) and individual solutions with 100 mg l$^{-1}$ Pb and 100 mg l$^{-1}$ Cd. The water hyacinth plants were left to grow for 240 h or until complete wilting occurred.

The total volume of the solution in each glass box was kept constant by adding deionized water to compensate for water lost through plant transpiration and evaporation.

[M. E. Soltan and M. N. Rashed, Laboratory study on the survival of water hyacinth under several conditions of heavy metal concentrations, *Advances in Environmental Research*, Volume 7, Issue 2, January 2003, 321-334.]

**TASK 11** *Reordering a Methods section*

It is important for a reader to be able to read the method as a logical sequence of steps. This task will give you practice in putting a sequence in its correct order.

The following is a jumbled summary of the Methods section of a student research paper. The writer's topic is: *Can living organisms survive in Hudson River water?* Her hypothesis was that the Daphnia will not be able to survive, not even in the lowest concentration of Hudson River water.

Read the sentences and reorder them into a logical sequence (write '1' alongside the first, and so on).

...... After placing the appropriate water concentrations and Daphnia in each beaker, they were stored in a safe and neutral place.

...... Beakers were stored for 1 hour, then 24 hours and concluded in 48 hours.

....... Finally, the 100% beaker was filled with 0ml of Hudson River water and 5ml of Daphnia culture water.

...... Next, the 50% beaker was filled with 5ml of Hudson River water, 5ml of spring water and 5ml of Daphnia culture water.

...... The control was filled up with 10ml of spring water with an additional 5ml of Daphnia culture water.

...... Three beakers were labelled with these solution concentrations (control, 50% and 100%).

## The Reality Principle

An important principle to keep in mind when writing is **the Reality Principle** – assume that your reader has a knowledge of the world and does not have to be told everything. Of course, everything depends on who your reader is. If you are writing for a scientific community you can assume an understanding of common scientific terms and procedures. However, if you are writing for a general readership you have to make different assumptions.

**TASK 12** *Applying the Reality Principle to a text*

You are going to read the first part of the methods section of a research paper entitled: *Unusual swimbladder behavior of fish in the Cariaco Trench* in order to determine **what information the reader is assumed to have in advance** of reading the article, and what information the reader is given.

Read '3 Methods' below, and then tick the appropriate boxes in the table.

| Information | Assumed | Given |
|---|---|---|
| 1  The location of the Cariaco Trench. | | |
| 2  Where in the Trench the measurements were taken. | | |
| 3  The depth of the ocean where the measurements were taken. | | |
| 4  What benign weather is like. | | |
| 5  The timing of sunset and sunrise. | | |

# **3** Methods

The experiment was conducted from 18 January through 3 February 1979 in the center of the western sub-basin of the Cariaco Trench. Measurements were within 10 km of 10°40′N, 65°30′W. Water depths were about 1400 m. Extensive acoustic and biological measurements were made but water chemistry was not examined.

Weather was benign during the experiment. Winds were usually less than 7 m/s, and never exceeded 10 m/s. Seas were usually less than 2 m and never exceeded 3 m. Sunrise barely changed, from 0645 to 0646, and sunset changed from 1820 to 1826 over the course of the experiment.

Now read '3.1 Acoustic measurements', then tick the appropriate boxes in the table below.

| Information | Assumed | Given |
|---|---|---|
| 6 For how long the acoustic measurements were taken. | | |
| 7 When they were taken. | | |
| 8 What type of ship was used. | | |
| 9 What a directional receiver is. | | |
| 10 What an array is. | | |
| 11 What a 32 element line hydrophone is. | | |
| 12 What ideal beam widths are. | | |

## 3.1 Acoustic measurements

Four acoustic measurement sequences totalling 48 h were conducted; two bracketing sunrise and two bracketing sunset. Volume scattering data were collected near the hour and half hour during all sequences. Scattering measurements used an explosive sound source and a directional receiver. A 0.23 kg TNT charge electrically detonated at 0.5 m depth provided a high source level over a broad frequency range.

Measurements were made while the ship slowly drifted, so that the tethered charges could drift 10–20 m from the ship before they were detonated.

Scattered signals were received by a downward-looking array deployed at 10 m, just below the hull of the ship. The array consisted of a 32 element line hydrophone on the axis of a 45° reflective cone of 1.8 m aperture. By listening to the upper 8, 16, or all 32 elements, ideal beam widths could be maintained between approximately 10° and 20° between 20 and 2.5 kHz.

[Love R.H., Fisher R.A., Wilson M.A., Nero R.W.,'Unusual swimbladder behavior of fish in the Cariaco Trench', *Deep Sea Research Part I: Oceanographic Research Papers*, January 2004, vol. 51, no. 1, pp 1–16), Publisher: Elsevier Science.]

..........................

**TASK 13** *Using the Reality Principle in your own writing*

Use an Internet search engine (Google, Google Scholar Ask Jeeves, etc.) to find a research paper on an aspect of the environment that interests you. Using the research paper as your reference, write an article for the general readership of a serious newspaper. Remember to apply the **reality principle** – assume that your reader has a knowledge of the world and does not have to be told everything. However, also bear in mind that your reader is not an expert in environmental studies. Your article should be between 350 and 500 words. Include graphics if they will help convey your meaning.

Your teacher will not mark or grade this article, but will give you some feedback on how effectively you are applying the Reality Principle.

## The writing process: Giving and getting formal peer feedback

You practised peer review in Unit 6. In this unit you are going to practise giving peer feedback using *criteria* to focus what you say, and what you hear from your peer(s). You will be asked to think about *what* criteria you would like your peer to apply to your writing.

In the next unit (Unit 8) you will have to be ready to have your writing evaluated on the criteria decided by your teacher.

**TASK 14** *Writing a text for peer review*

Describe a process you are familiar with, using enough detail (the reality principle) for another person to be able to use your methods to follow the same process. Write for a non-specialist reader. Write at least 500 words. Your essay should show evidence that you have researched your topic using printed materials and the Internet.

When you have a first draft ready, you should ask three peers to review your text using the peer review form in Task 15 below. You could look again at Appendix A.

**TASK 15**

*Carrying out peer review*

Look at the set of criteria in the peer review form on the next page: each of these criteria focuses on something that teachers often pay attention to when deciding what mark or grade a piece of writing deserves. The criteria focus on processes and methods (which you have just been studying) and your ability to apply coherence rules (which you have been practising). For other pieces of work, the criteria will be different.

Exchange essays with a peer. Read your peer's essay carefully, paying attention to one criterion at a time. For each of the criteria, place a tick in one of the evaluation boxes; **also** write helpful comments to support your evaluation. Notice that you may not find all the aspects of the essay equally good or poor.

When you write your feedback:
- be polite and respectful of the writer's feelings

## Peer Review Form

| Criteria | Very good | Satisfactory | Needs to do more work | Comments |
|---|---|---|---|---|
| **Organisation**: paragraphs, ideas well arranged for the reader | | | | |
| **Clarity**: explanation of methods/processes | | | | |
| **Vocabulary**: especially accuracy of nominalisations | | | | |
| Quality of **grammar**, **spelling** and **punctuation** | | | | |

- make sure your comments can be understood by the writer
- be constructive, not destructive.

Now exchange essays with another peer and repeat the process. Finally, exchange essays with a third peer and repeat the process.

**TASK 16** *Reviewing your own writing*

Before you read any of your peers' feedback, use the peer review criteria above to evaluate **your own** text (this is called 'self-evaluation'). Use a photocopy or second computer copy of the peer review form to write comments to yourself. Remember to *read* your writing (even though you wrote it, you might see some new strong or weak areas); and pay attention to each criterion, one at a time, before evaluating yourself.

**TASK 17** *Making use of peer review feedback*

1 Now read your partners' feedback; and compare their feedback with your own review of your essay.
2 Decide which areas you need to improve and make the improvements.
3 Submit the improved essay to your teacher with a note showing what feedback suggestions you made use of. Your teacher will judge you on the final result, but will pay attention to what feedback you used and how, and may have advice for you for the future.

# Results, discussion and academic relevance

This unit aims to improve your writing skills by:

1. examining thesis statements and arguments
2. showing how to put the concept of coherence into practice
3. examining key aspects of the results section of a paper
4. introducing the Relevance Principle
5. examining key aspects of the discussion section of a paper
6. helping you to develop your own academic voice.

## What is an argument?

Much of the work done by academics involves understanding, reporting and interpreting the work of others. But **knowledge** is created by original research, and original research requires original thinking. If someone is to think originally, they have to think **critically** and be able to argue.

The academic argument begins with a statement (thesis) that is debatable: that is, an idea you believe in, but with which other people might disagree. The remainder of your text provides evidence *for* your thesis statements and *against* opposing arguments. Your aim is to convince your readers of the correctness of your thesis by providing evidence that *they* will find convincing and by defeating alternative arguments that *they* might have believed.

**TASK 1** *Identifying a thesis statement*

A thesis is a statement about which people can take different points of view – it is debatable. Study the following statements and decide which are theses (that is, which are debatable) and which are matters of fact. You will probably have to look up some of these in books or on the Internet to find out.

| Statement | Thesis | Factual |
|---|---|---|
| 1 With a tablespoon of blood, the DNA of an individual can determine the relatedness of individuals, families, tribal groups, and populations. | | |
| 2 If you cloned yourself, there is no guarantee that your clone would be just like you. | | |
| 3 The nematode Caenorhabditis elegans is among the most widely studied model organisms in current biological and biomedical research. | | |
| 4 We are what our genes make us. | | |
| 5 Genetically modified food will mainly benefit the world's poor. | | |
| 6 A gene is a discrete sequence of DNA nucleotides | | |

**TASK 2** *Identifying different kinds of evidence*

Having established a thesis statement, the academic writer's next step must be to determine what kind of academic evidence is needed to support the thesis. Academic evidence usually consists of data that is acceptable (as evidence) by the academic community.

The evidence you provide in support of your thesis statement may take a number of forms. It can consist of reasons and arguments based on expert opinion and research findings, case studies or facts and statistics. Thus in the field of genetics, evidence consists of genetic data produced in a manner acceptable to geneticists. The data are facts, but what facts *mean* needs to be interpreted and since data is open to multiple interpretations, arguments are needed to convince the community that one interpretation is superior to all others.

Study the thesis statements below and the evidence that supports them. Decide what kind of evidence (**A** to **F**) is being offered.

A reasons          D case study

B research findings     E facts

C examples          F statistics

| Thesis Statements | Evidence |
|---|---|
| 1 While it is possible that someone will clone an entire basketball team of Michael Jordans, such a team will not necessarily be winners. | What people don't understand is that with cloning you're creating twins, and like identical twins that occur naturally, they are not necessarily identical in the sense of personality. <br> http://www.princetoninfo.com/clone.html |

| | |
|---|---|
| 2 Insulin-dependent diabetes (IDDM) has been described in all racial groups but its incidence varies almost 60-fold between countries. Does the variation in incidence reflect differences in genetic susceptibility or environmental influences? | The Mediterranean island of Sardinia has the second highest incidence of childhood-onset IDDM in the world (30.2 per 100 000 per year). This ranking is in striking contrast to the low incidence (6.5) in Lazio, a region of neighbouring mainland Italy, and to the general trend in Europe of a reducing incidence of IDDM as one moves South from Scandinavia. Muntoni and colleagues report that the incidence of IDDM in children born in Lazio to parents of Sardinian origin was fourfold higher than the incidence in children born to parents from mainland Italy. Children with one parent of Sardinian origin had intermediate risk. http://www.diabetolognytt.nu/forum/messages/122.html retrieved 17/10/03 |
| 3 Benefits of genetic testing | At BYU, Scott Woodward, director of the Molecular Genealogy Research Group, and research assistants are collaborating to construct a global genetic database to be used for genealogical purposes. When the database is complete, people will be able to trace their genealogical lines through their genes. This type of linking will help identify persons who are unable to be identified by traditional methods. This technology will also allow identification of those involved in cases such as rapes and murders where DNA samples are available. http://newsnet.byu.edu/story.cfm/35000 retrieved 17/10/03 |
| 4 While genetic research can determine the heritability of some diseases, the genetic foundations of behaviour are much more difficult to identify. | From a genetic point of view, physical traits, such as the colour of a person's hair, have a much higher heritability than behaviour. In fact, behaviour genetics assumes that the genetic bases of an individual's behaviour simply cannot be determined. Consequently, researchers have focused their efforts on the behaviour of groups, particularly families. However, even controlled studies of families have failed to establish conclusive links between genetics and behaviour, or between genetics and particular psychological traits and aptitudes. In theory, these links probably exist; in practice, however, researchers have been unable to isolate traits that are unmodified by environmental factors. http://wwwfindarticles.com/cf. o/g2699/0002/269900233/p1/article.html?term= nature+nurture+controversy retrieved 17/10/03 |

| | |
|---|---|
| 5 The decision to create a national health and genetic information database in Iceland has spurred a considerable amount of controversy. | At the time the Act on Health Sector Database 139/1998 was passed, public opinion polls (see http://www.iceland.org/) revealed that 20–25% of Icelanders had serious reservations about deCODE and the federal government's plan to build the database. Sigmundur Gudbjarnason, a biochemistry professor at the University of Iceland, stated, 'It ignores the rights of privacy and patient's rights. It will turn Decode into a scientific monopoly. The main body of concern is focused on the fact that the database will amass a large amount of personal and potentially sensitive information in one readily accessible computer system.'<br><br>http:www.molbio.princeton.edu/courses/mb427/<br>1999/projects/990s/ethics.htm retrieved 17/10/03 |

**TASK 3** *Identifying an argument*

A written argument is a text that:

1 lays out a position, a recognised set of views in the discipline
2 attempts to show why it is wrong or incomplete.

The creation of the research gap, which you learned about in Unit 3, is a specific form of argument.

Read A to C texts. State which of them you consider to be an argument based on the criteria given in 1 and 2 above.

**Text A  Education for all**

Education ministers and representatives from 52 Commonwealth countries are meeting in Edinburgh this week to discuss ways of improving access to education for all children around the world. Ministers from as far afield as Botswana, Zambia, Malaysia and Papua New Guinea will join England's education secretary, Charles Clarke, and Scotland's first minister, Jack McConnell, in Edinburgh for the four-day conference. A parallel forum for youth delegates from all the participating countries will run alongside the main event.

Ministers' discussions will focus on six areas, including achieving universal primary education, tackling gender disparities in education and mitigating the effects of HIV/Aids on education systems. Fringe events will include one organised by developmental charity Oxfam, which is campaigning for equal access to education for girls around the world.

http://education.guardian.co.uk/higher/worldwide/story retrieved 29/9/03

### Text B  Why Clone?

Research advances over the past decade have told us that, with a little work, we humans can clone just about anything we want, from frogs to monkeys and probably even ourselves!

But why would we want to clone things? One of the most controversial applications of cloning is of human stem cells. Stem cells are the body's building blocks, responsible for developing, maintaining and repairing the body throughout life. As a result, they might be used to repair damaged or diseased organs and tissues. Researchers are currently looking toward cloning as a way to create genetically defined human stem cells for research and medical purposes. They hope that cloning would reduce the ethical concerns many people have about using actual human stem cells. To learn more about cloning stem cells, go to

http://gslc.genetics.utah.edu/units/cloning/clonezone/clnav.cfm retrieved 21-3-04

### Text C  Nature or nurture?

Current thinking in biology discredits the notion that genes alone can determine a trait because genes are never sufficient in isolation. Rather, particular genes influence the development of a trait in the context of a particular environment. Thus, measurements of the degree to which a trait is influenced by genes versus environment will depend on the particular environment and genes examined. In many cases, it has been found that genes may have a substantial contribution to psychological traits, such as intelligence and personality; yet these traits may be largely influenced by environment in other circumstances.

http://en.wikipedia.org/wiki/Nature_versus_nurture: retrieved 21-3-04

## The language of argument

In Units 6 and 7 you worked on factual material and on the language needed for writing about facts and data – events, processes, and so on. You will use that language again in 'The Results and Discussion sections' part of this unit (page 111). But first, let us look at a different kind of language – the language of argument.

Academics often write arguments because they are writing about subjects that are controversial. In 1600, relativity was unknown; in 1800, it was still a controversial theory. In 1100, everyone believed that the Earth was flat; when some people tried to revive the flat earth theory in the 20th century, they were ridiculed. Knowledge changes, and it changes because of research. New thinking becomes known and accepted because of effective argument. And language is vital to effective argument.

Certain verbs and adverbs, as well as formulaic phrases, are frequently used in writing arguments.

*Table 8.1 Verbs, adverbs and formulaic phrases used in arguments*

**Argumentative verbs**
Pro: believe, think, prove
Con: doubt, question

**Emotionally-charged boosters**
particularly, definitely, certainly, surprising

**Personalisation (when arguing your own position)**
I/we/our; this group includes most of the argumentative verbs (e.g. We believe that …)

**Formulaic phrases**
In my opinion, beyond a doubt, a serious flaw

**De-personalisations (when criticising others)**
such as 'the findings may be criticised …' (Note: the findings are criticised – not the researchers), 'it is unjustified to …'

**TASK 4** *Increasing the argumentative level*
The following abstract of a study about whether twins will both give up smoking or not is written in a highly factual way, without any argumentative language. Choose three sentences in the text and rewrite them using some of the argumentative language presented in Table 8.1 above.

# Genetics of Smoking – A Study of Male Twins

## Abstract

BACKGROUND: This study examined the effects of genetics on smoking behavior.

METHODS: We conducted a genetic analysis of several aspects of smoking behavior among subjects in the National Academy of Sciences' National Research Council Twin Registry. The registry includes male twins who were born in the United States between 1917 and 1927 and who were members of the armed forces during World War II. Information on smoking history was available for 4,775 pairs of twins, who were first surveyed in 1967 through 1969, when they were 40 to 50 years old, and then resurveyed in 1983 through 1985, when they were 56 to 66. Eighty percent of the subjects in this cohort had smoked at some time in their lives, 60% were smokers in 1967 through 1969, and 39% were smoking in 1983 through 1985. Similarities between twins in smoking habits at baseline and at the second follow-up 16 years later were examined. Smoking behavior for identical and non-identical twins was compared to assess the relative contribution of familial and genetic factors.

RESULTS: In the 1967–69 survey, the ratio of observed to expected concordance for smoking was higher among identical twins than among the non-identical twins for those who had never smoked (overall rate ratio, 1.38; 95% confidence interval, 1.25 to 1.54), for former smokers (overall rate ratio, 1.59; 95% confidence interval, 1.35 to 1.85), for current cigarette smokers (overall rate ratio, 1.18; 95% confidence interval, 1.11 to 1.26), and for current cigar or pipe smokers (overall rate ratio, 1.60; 95% confidence interval, 1.22 to 2.06). The data also suggest genetic influences on quitting smoking. Identical twins were more likely than non-identical twins to both quit smoking (overall rate ratio, 1.24; 95% confidence interval, 1.06 to 1.45).

CONCLUSIONS: In this cohort of adult male twins, there were moderate genetic influences on lifetime smoking practices.

G. Swan, D. Carmelli, D. Robinette & R. Fabsitz.
http://www.sri.com/policy/healthsci/addiction/genetics.html Retrieved 9-11-04

## TASK 5 *Checking for coherence in an argument*

It is also important in writing an argument to make clear the links (connections) between concepts and details. Study the underlined connectives in the text below, then put each into the appropriate column in the grid according to the type of relationship (support, contrast, etc.) they have with the main argument.

| Support | Contrast | Conclude | Add weight | Show caution |
|---------|----------|----------|------------|--------------|
|         |          |          |            |              |

Although genetic research can determine the heritability of some diseases, the genetic foundations of behaviour are much more difficult to identify. For one thing, from a genetic point of view, physical traits, such as the colour of a person's hair, have a much higher heritability than behaviour. In fact, behaviour genetics assumes that the genetic bases of an *individual's* behaviour simply cannot be determined. Consequently, researchers have focused their efforts on the behaviour of groups, particularly families. However, even controlled studies of families have failed to establish conclusive links between genetics and behaviour, or indeed between genetics and particular psychological traits and aptitudes. It would seem that in theory, these links probably exist; in practice, however, researchers have been unable to isolate traits that are unmodified by environmental factors. For example, musical aptitude seems to recur in certain families. While it is tempting to assume that this aptitude is an inherited genetic trait, it would be a mistake to ignore the environment. Hence what is colloquially known as 'talent' is probably a combination of genetic and other, highly variable, factors.

Adapted from: http://www.findarticles.com/cf_0/g2699/0002/2699000233/p1/article.jhtml?term=nature+nuture retrieved 17/10/03

**TASK 6** *Presenting an academic identity*

The text below contains many cases of **personalisation**. Rewrite the text so that it is less personal, but still reads as an argument.

> In my opinion, becoming a strong writer calls for a blend of inherent ability and skills that are learned. I believe that the 'closed capacities' (Foster 180) are skills that can be trained and that any intelligent person will master. But I doubt whether the 'open capacities' such as good discourse structure and style can be taught or learned. I am often surprised by how many people say they have had a writing course and yet still can't create a good essay.
>
> Although we can't prove it yet, it seems to me beyond a doubt that you need more than good skills in the closed capacities to become a good writer. I think that people who have learned how to write a clear and accurate five paragraph essay with an introductory paragraph, three main body paragraphs with some support in each, and a concluding paragraph, can definitely learn to develop their open capacities and become good at invention, arrangement/organisation, and self-revision by practice and plenty of reading. I know I did.

**TASK 7** *Giving academic support*

With what you have learned from the preceding texts, look at sentences 1 to 4. Write another sentence to follow each of them, giving some support/evidence so that it is more acceptable as an **academic** argument.

1 Cloning is a technique that makes the replication of a person without sexual reproduction scientifically possible.
2 All humans within the range of normal intelligence have the potential to learn to talk.
3 The availability of universal education is a key goal of the United Nations.
4 Research on twins separated from birth shows the importance of the home environment on their personality development.

## The Results and Discussion sections

It is easy to confuse the Results and Discussion sections of research papers. The simplest way to think about the difference is to remember that *R* = *R*, that is, Results = Reporting.

## *Results*

Raw data include all observations or data that you get from your experiment. Raw data are never included in your scientific paper unless they are needed to give evidence for specific conclusions which cannot be obtained by looking at an analysis, or summation, of the data. You present converted data in your report, as figures (graphs), tables, and/or descriptions of observations. You need to present your converted data well, in order to make your point succinctly and clearly.

In a research essay, report or academic paper, the Results section describes but does not interpret your results. Its function is to provide the reader with a clear description of your findings. You can draw attention to data you think are very important or constitute trends. Here is an example, from the *Journal of the Society for Gynaecological Investigation* Vol. 7, No. 4 (2000). Note that the numbers in square brackets relate to the Reference list, using the referencing conventions of medicine.

# Perinatal mortality

Twins have perinatal mortality rates fivefold to tenfold higher than singletons. [9 and 29] Reported fetal death rates are threefold to fivefold higher [7 and 9] and neonatal death rates fivefold to sevenfold higher for twin gestations compared with singletons. [9 and 28] Despite this, twins have better weight-specific survival rates than singletons, particularly among low birth weight infants. [16 and 30] Weight-specific perinatal mortality rates for singletons and twins in the United States (1995 and 1996) are shown in Table 4.

*Table 4. Birth Weight-Specific Perinatal Mortality Rates (PMR) in Singletons and Twins in the United States, 1995–1996*

**States, 1995–1996**

| Birth weight (g) | Singletons | | Twins | | Relative risk |
|---|---|---|---|---|---|
| | Total births | PMR | Total births | PMR | |
| 500–999 | 25.852 | 714.3 | 5.120 | 638.5 | 0.9 |
| 1000–1499 | 51.120 | 364.5 | 10.266 | 298.9 | 0.8 |
| 1500–1999 | 45.968 | 133.9 | 11.288 | 63.5 | 0.5 |
| 2000–2499 | 86.256 | 65.7 | 26.392 | 19.1 | 0.3 |
| 2500–2999 | 296.640 | 19.6 | 58.784 | 6.5 | 0.3 |
| 3000–3499 | 1,212.416 | 5.0 | 61.880 | 3.2 | 0.6 |
| 3500–3999 | 2,830.336 | 2.0 | 25.676 | 3.4 | 1.7 |
| 4000–4499 | 2,238.976 | 1.4 | 3.842 | 4.9 | 3.5 |
| >4500 | 795.440 | 2.0 | 394 | 9.2 | 4.7 |

:········· :

**TASK 8** *Understanding which data to use in an argument*
Write labels on Table 4 (above) to show which figures are for the
highest level of twins mortality and for singleton mortality. Identify
any points in the table where twins have a better survival rate than
singletons.

:········· :

**TASK 9** *Describing the data to use in an argument*
When you write the Results section, rather than just putting a table
(or other visual data display) in the paper and then moving on to
the discussion section, you need to describe the relationship of each
section of converted data to the overall study. For example look at
Table 1-E below, which you worked with in Task 5 of Unit 3.

*Table 1-E – Incomes and food prices*

| Country | 1998 GNP per capital (constant 1995 $US) | Average growth rate of GNP per capita, 1994–96 | Bread and cereal price index 1998 (PPP) | Meat Price Index 1998 (PPP) |
|---|---|---|---|---|
| **United States** | 29,316 | 2.66 | 100 | 100 |
| **EU** | | | | |
| Austria | 30,841 | 2.21 | 114 | 163 |
| Belgium | 29,284 | 2.36 | 116 | 161 |
| Denmark | 36,892 | 3.30 | 156 | 210 |
| Finland | 27,807 | 5.23 | 147 | 156 |
| France | 28,028 | 2.19 | 125 | 157 |
| Germany | 30,941 | 1.65 | 145 | 187 |
| Greece | 12,111 | 2.32 | 104 | 102 |
| Ireland | 19,469 | 7.78 | 80 | 103 |
| Italy | 19,363 | 1.68 | 101 | 135 |
| Luxembourg | 50,851 | 1.22 | NA | NA |
| Netherlands | 28,344 | 2.81 | 106 | 176 |
| Portugal | 11,573 | 2.82 | 85 | 116 |
| Spain | 15,405 | 2.66 | 89 | 91 |
| Sweden | 26,613 | 2.34 | 151 | 179 |
| United Kingdom | 20,214 | 2.72 | 90 | 128 |

http://www.ers.usda.gov/publications/WRS0404/WRS0404f.pdf extracted 17/10/03

Now look at the explanatory text provided with the text (below).

Table 1-E gives purchasing power parity indices between food prices in the countries
considered here. A quantity of bread and cereal items that would cost $100 in the US would
cost $156 in Denmark but only $90 in the United Kingdom and only $80 in Ireland. Meat

costs are higher in most European countries than in the US. A quantity of meat costing $100 in the US would cost $210 in Denmark, but only $91 in Spain.

In 1997, US consumers spent only 3.8% of average household income on food, whereas European Union countries spent an average of 17.4% of family income on food in the same period.

Using the data in Table 1-E above, write a short text (a paragraph or two) comparing food prices in Spain with those in Germany.

## Discussion

In this section, you must explain, analyse, and interpret your results, being especially careful to explain any errors or problems. You need to explain all your results, although you may discuss some of them more fully than others. This is one of many times when the Relevance Principle becomes important.

**The Relevance Principle**
The last of the four principles of good writing is the Relevance Principle, which reminds us to keep to our topic and our purpose in writing.

**TASK 10** *Ensuring relevance*
In Task 9 you wrote a Results section comparing food prices in two of the countries. Look at the Discussion section below, which a student wrote to follow the Results text of Task 9. With a partner, decide which parts of the text do not conform to the Relevance Principle, and put a line through them (like this). If necessary, write some replacement text of your own that discusses the results without breaking the Relevance Principle.

The results reported show that the purchasing power of different countries in Europe varies greatly. A family in Denmark or Germany will need to spend much more on bread and cereals than a family in Portugal or Greece. In Austria and Belgium the purchasing power is almost exactly the same. Further, a family in Denmark or Germany will need to spend even more on meat than in Portugal or Greece. Information about Luxembourg was not available. Meat costs are higher in every European country except Spain than in the US. The countries that will find it most difficult to afford meat are Portugal and Greece.

*Using connectives*

The connectives used in the Discussion section of research papers are all familiar, but we use them with a different purpose, as Table 8.2 shows.

Table 8.2 Useful connectives for the Discussion section

| Sequence | Purpose |
| --- | --- |
| Firstly/First First of all | Used to introduce the first (usually most important) finding |
| Secondly,/Second, Thirdly,/Third, etc. | Used to introduce the second (third, etc.) result of importance |
| In addition Furthermore Moreover | Used for any added results that build up the argument about what the Results mean |
| However | Used to introduce discussion of any result which contradicts an argument that has been built up |
| Finally | Signals that this is the last result that will be discussed |
| In conclusion Thus | Used to generalise from all the supporting arguments, e.g. *Thus it is clear from the arguments presented that the genetic bases of an individual's behaviour simply cannot be determined.* |

Use an appropriate connective from Table 8.2 to fill in the blanks in the following text.

Previous studies have shown that although, in general, twins have higher perinatal mortality rates than singletons, this is not true in all conditions. This large-scale controlled study investigated whether this paradoxical situation is due to (1) gestational age distribution differences between the singleton and twin populations, or (2) the increased likelihood of birth having occurred in an advanced perinatal centre.

_____, this study's findings confirm the lower mortality of preterm twins. _____, after controlling for level of hospital of birth this difference remained, suggesting that birth in an advanced perinatal centre was not a major factor responsible for the twin advantage. _____, the study confirmed previous findings that preterm twins have lower mortality than singletons at the same gestation. _____, analyses in which gestational age was standardized indicate that, for those whose gestational age was less than 2 SD below the mean for their particular group (twin or singleton), twins were at higher risk than singletons.

_____, the results support earlier authors' suggestions that the definition of term birth should be different for twins and singletons.

Adapted from J.C. Payne et al, *Perinatal Mortality in Term and Preterm Twin and Singleton Births,* Twin Research Vol 5, No 4.

When you refer to information, remember to distinguish between: data generated by your own studies; information from published sources; and information obtained from other students, as the authors of the text above have done.

## TASK 12 *Suggesting future research*

The best research studies open up new avenues of research. When you finish your discussion of the data and findings, ask yourself: What questions remain? Did the study lead me to any new questions? Then try to think up a new hypothesis and briefly suggest new experiments to further address the main question.

1 With a partner or small group, discuss what research might usefully be done into defining term birth appropriately for twins.
2 Write one or two sentences to make a final paragraph for the discussion text in Task 11.

You will find the hedges and boosters you studied in Unit 5 useful when writing suggestions for future research.

## TASK 13 *Using the correct tenses in discussion*

In writing and academic discussion there are some general 'rules' for the use of tenses that are helpful to remember.
• Refer to work done by specific individuals (including yourself) in the past tense.
• Refer to generally accepted facts and principles in the present tense.
• Refer to work that you will build your own work on in the present perfect tense.

Correct the tenses marked in **bold** in the extract below.

Many twin studies (1) **made use of** identical twins (who (2) **had** the same genetic makeup) who were raised in differing environments in order to control for genetic effects: that is, any variation between twins (3) **was** clearly attributable to the environment, allowing the researcher to quantify the effects of the environment by measuring variance of a trait between twins. Identical twins (4) **had raised** separately may have experienced quite different environments; yet many studies (5) **have often been found** that they live similar lives, have similar personalities and similar levels of intelligence. On the other hand, even identical twins who (6) **been raised** together often differ in significant ways.

[Adapted from http://en.wikipedia.org/wiki/Nature_versus_nurture: Retrieved 21-3-04]

# The writing process: Finding an academic voice

**TASK 14** *Getting peer feedback on your academic voice*
You will be writing about this topic:

---

The prospect of cloning humans is highly controversial and raises a number of ethical, legal and social challenges that need to be considered. Find out what some of these issues are within the University of Utah website (http://gslc.genetics.utah.edu/units/cloning/clonezone/clnav.cfm), or visit any others.

---

Your teacher may ask you to work through a writing process in class time, or you can do this yourself with a group of peers. By this stage in the course you should be developing an idea of what writing processes work well for you.

Bring to class a reasonably complete draft of a paper, about 500–650 words in length, on the subject of the ethics of cloning. In a small group, carry out peer review **focusing your commentary on the academic voice of the writer.**

---

## Peer Review Form: Part One

Does the writer clearly define a thesis statement?

Does each paragraph present a different aspect of the topic?

Are supporting arguments and evidence present, and clearly stated?

Are arguments and evidence relevant?

Are credible opposing arguments acknowledged?

Are the opposing arguments rebutted?

---

Part One of the Peer Review Form covers the basics, and you should make sure that you succeed fairly well on all these areas. Make notes of your peers' comments so that you can revise your writing later. Now work together with the second peer review form on the next page.

## Peer Review Form: Part Two

Is other people's research reported objectively?

If other people's research is <u>not</u> reported objectively, are accepted academic forms of subjectivity – such as hedging, boosting and modality expressions – used properly?

Are arguments and support clearly connected so that the reader can focus on the meaning and not the language?

Does the writer's own position on this issue come across? Point out the places where the writer succeeds in doing that, and the places where she or he fails.

Does the writer convince you of the reasonableness of his or her position?

**TASK 15** *Writing task*

**Revise your draft:** Use the feedback you got from your peers to revise your writing. As you revise, think about the criteria you worked with in Unit 7: organisation, clarity, vocabulary, and language (grammar, spelling and punctuation). Also remember the four Principles you have learned: Clarity, Honesty, Reality and Relevance.

Add another important criterion to your thinking about your own writing: does the text fulfil the task? (In other words, does it do what the instructor wanted and expected? Does it satisfy you that you have done all you can to make your writing correct, informative, and interesting?) This is a hard criterion to define, but it has regularly been found in research to be extremely important to readers, whether these are language teachers or academic lecturers.

This writing will be graded by your teacher using the criteria referred to above and any others that are decided; you will be told what these criteria are before you begin your revision.

# UNIT 9 The whole academic text

This unit aims to improve your writing skills by:

1. examining techniques for organising a text
2. introducing a structure for writing introductions
3. exploring ways to make text more coherent
4. showing you how to make effective use of teacher evaluation.

## S-P-S-E: Focus on structure

**TASK 1** *Recognising a text structure*
The paragraphs of the text below and on page 120 have been disorganised; number the paragraphs to show the correct order.

# Solving the world's educational problems

**A**
Investment in the educational system needs to increase and take on more creative forms. Problem populations such as rural, minority, nomadic, poor, female or abandoned children should be targeted. Schools can be designed to accommodate non-formal learning, cultural events and community activities. The growing role of television and non-traditional mediums of learning should be recognized. Supplemental increases in health care, food intake and sanitation will amplify the beneficial effects of education. The following two successful and cost-effective examples show that the world's educational problems can be solved.

**B**
Only 10% reach fifth grade. Due to absenteeism, it takes an average of ten years instead of five to finish fifth grade in Cambodia. Populations in remote, rural areas tend to have low educational attainment levels and little access to educational resources. Seasonal absence from school is normal in agricultural areas as farm families need children's labor at harvest or planting time. Rural or poor areas have little political power and thus get the least educational resources. Teachers are often not willing to go to these remote areas which lack modern conveniences.

**C**

The Bangladesh Rural Advancement Committee has an educational project that reaches children who never enrolled in school, who dropped out, or who came from landless families. Nigeria has built an educational program specifically for children of nomads. There are currently over 610 schools with more than 42,000 students in this program. Both of these efforts need to be replicated throughout the developing world.

**D**

School systems in the developing world have expanded rapidly in the last three decades. After independence from colonialism, most developing countries inherited educational systems which were designed for a small elite and civil servants. School enrolment rates went up from 100 million in 1950 to 600 million in 1980. However, the socio-economic and political climate in developing countries is responsible for serious shortcomings in the educational systems. Of the 300 million children in the world who do not attend school, most live in developing areas. Civil strife and war are responsible for destroying educational infrastructure and resources in some countries. For example, in Cambodia, few of the 40,000 pre-1979 primary school teachers survived the political massacres of the 1970s. Population growth increases exponentially the need for educational infrastructure. In Venezuela, 800,000 school children entered the educational system in 1958. In 1992, 8 million entered.

Adapted from Global Issues primer: http://www.osearth.com/resources/recall/ed.shtml visited 22/11/03

The reason you found it relatively easy to reorder the text is that it follows a common way of organising texts: Situation, Problem, Solution and Evaluation (S-P-S-E).

**Situation** answers the question:
*'What are we talking about?'*
School systems in the developing world

**Problem** answers the question:
*'What is problematic about this?'*
Too many students do not complete their education

**Solution** answers the question:
*'What is to be done about it?'*
More creative investments in education

**Evaluation** answers the question:
*'How good is the solution?'*
It worked in Bangladesh and Nigeria

**TASK 2** *Recognising details of the S-P-S-E text structure*
Read the text below and write very brief notes to complete this
diagram.

| | |
|---|---|
| **Situation**: | girls face educational discrimination – millions kept out of schools. |
| **Problem**: | |
| **Solution(s)**: | |
| **Evaluation**: | |

# Girls Continue to Face Inequity in Education Worldwide, says UN Report

The latest UN report on education says girls face sharp discrimination in access to education, which means millions of them are kept out of school. The report says the lack of gender parity in education is an important obstacle to social and economic progress.

In many developing countries, particularly in South Asia and sub-Saharan Africa, there are only seven girls in primary school for every 10 boys. In the world's two most populous countries, India and China, boys continue to outnumber girls in schools. The annual Education for All report by UNESCO says the proportion of girls in school did rise slightly in the past decade. But more than half of the 104 million children out of school are still females, making gender parity in education a distant goal in more than 50 countries. The UN says that in many countries, high school fees, early marriage, and economic pressure to put children to work early, block girls from school.

Christopher Colclough, the Paris-based director for the Education for All report, is calling for a change in the cultural and social values that keep girls out of school, particularly in poor countries.

"The poor countries in the world tend to be the ones in which the social norms and values of society are most tolerant of inequality, and where the roles of men and women in society are more sharply different," he said. "Parents give different opportunities and different resources to boys and girls stemming from those different values."

The United Nations is calling for countries to make primary education free, and reduce the dependence of poor households on child labor to ensure that more girls get into school. It says educating girls has a high payoff by increasing household incomes and reducing poverty. Mr. Colclough also is asking countries to adopt innovative methods to help girls stay in school. He cites the example of one of the world's poorest countries, Bangladesh, where several programs have helped tens-of-thousands of poor girls reach secondary school.

"It is being done both by very imaginative approaches to school expansion, which have emphasized the role of women teachers, emphasized flexibility in terms of the school timetable, and also by the introduction of scholarships … which have been focused on the poor," he said.

http://www.voanews.com/article.cfm?objectID=545388A3-9A35-498C-9CCBF8AAF5D7789A# visited 07/11/03

**TASK 3**  *Introducing a Problem section*

Here is the Situation section of an academic paper called: *Quality Education and Social Stratification: The Paradox of Private Schooling in China*. Read the text and complete the last sentence to show the beginning of the Problem section.

> Since the opening of the first elite private school in June 1992, private schools have mushroomed in China. By November 1996, there were more than 60,000 private institutions, hosting 6.8 million students (China Education Daily, 11/1/1996). Though the percentage of private schools is still less than 4 percent of all schools in China, the current boom in private schools, especially the primary and the secondary level ...............................
>
> ...............................................................................
>
> ...............................................................................
>
> ...............................................................................
>
> [Extracted from http://www.tc.columbia.edu/CICE/articles/hcbd112.htm visited 07/11/03]

**TASK 4**  *Completing a Solution section*

Here are the Situation and Problem sections of a report on education in Benin. Read the text and try to complete the Solution section that would follow (write a sentence or two).

# EDUCATION

# How Money Causes Problems ... and Opportunities: An Example from Benin

Often the path to improving the education system is not exactly a straight line.

Such has been the experience in Benin where the government, in the framework of the Poverty Reduction Strategy, announced an annual subsidy of about $3 per student for all of the country's nearly one million primary school students.

This sounds, of course, like a good thing. The money is provided to the schools and is meant to lighten the burden on parents who normally pay school fees amounting to about $2 per month. It helps schools to pay teachers and meet other needs such as books and furniture that always are in short supply.

The immediate result was a rush by parents to enrol children in schools as, in many cases, school directors abolished school fees in response to this act of social largesse. Overall, in fact, more than 140,000 additional children were enrolled in school last school year than in the year before.

But, as can happen, a positive measure turned out to have unforeseen consequences, at least in the beginning. One of these was that parents in some cases stopped contributing to help meet school costs on the grounds that the government was now providing a subsidy. Where this happened it meant schools ended up with less, rather than more, total funding. Another consequence was that some School Directors excluded parents' committees from participation in deciding how these funds were used, on the grounds that it was not their concern. This did nothing to improve overall management of the schools, or to ensure efficient use of the funds.

Though it is hard to say how widespread these problems were, they were real enough to prompt the USAID-funded PVO World Education to take action. It should be noted that World Education provides technical assistance to parents' associations so that they can play a more active role in the education system. Here was a golden opportunity to push the fledgling parents' associations into the political arena.

.............................................................................................................

.............................................................................................................

.............................................................................................................

[Extracted from http://www.usaid.gov/regions/afr/ss02/benin.html visited 07/11/03]

:<br>::::::::::::::::::::::::

**TASK 5** *Recognising signals for an Evaluation section*
Below are the Solution and Evaluation parts of the Benin text from Task 4. The Solution section is underlined. Read what comes after the Solution, then answer these questions.

1 How does the writer evaluate the solution: positively or negatively?
2 Which words/phrases show the writer's evaluation of the role of the FENAPEB?

**EDUCATION:** How Money Causes Problems … and Opportunities: An Example from Benin (*continued*)

Though it is hard to say how widespread these problems were, they were real enough to prompt the USAID-funded PVO World Education to take action. It should be noted that World Education provides technical assistance to parents' associations so that they can play a more active role in the education system. Here was a golden opportunity to push the fledgling parents' associations into the political arena. In response to this experience of mixed results, in September 2001 World Education organized a national meeting of parents' school committees to discuss their experiences related to the subsidy and to propose to the Ministry of Education measures to address these problems.

Following this meeting, the conclusions and recommendations were presented by the national association of parents' associations (FENAPEB) to the Minister of Education. In fact, this was the first political action taken by FENAPEB, whose members are being trained by World Education with a grant from USAID. Soon afterwards, the Minister of Education issued a policy decree largely based on the FENAPEB recommendations and clarifying the role of the parents' associations in managing the subsidy funds. Since the start of the 2001–2002 school year, this new policy has been applied throughout Benin. Initial indications are that it has helped to settle the situation by providing guidelines on the role of the parents' associations in determining the use of the subsidy.

It has also, it should be noted, given FENAPEB a seat at the table in policy dialogue with the Ministry. Since their initial success, FENAPEB now participates regularly in such discussions, which is an important step forward in building a partnership between government and civil society to manage the educational system in Benin.

[Extracted from http://www.usaid.gov/regions/afr/ss02/benin.html visited 7/11/03]

**TASK 6** *Using the S-P-S-E structure to write a plan for an essay*
Write brief notes for an essay plan on one of these topics. Use the Situation–Problem–Solution–Evaluation structure.

# Parents' roles in children's education

# Technology in education

# Studying abroad

# Education in our secondary schools

## S-P-S-E in the Introduction

······················
:·

**TASK 7** *Recognising the S-P-S-E structure in the introduction to a text*

Read the introduction to an essay below. Then match each sentence to one of the four parts of the Introduction structure which follows.

---

### Parents can make a major contribution in their children's schools

The question of parental involvement in schools is a relatively modern phenomenon. In the past, parents sent their children to school and largely left it to the school to educate them as it saw fit. While this arrangement was widely respected, it is no longer a model for educational arrangements today. Nowadays, parents see themselves as providing the finances for schools whether they be private or public and as financiers they are demanding a say in what happens in the schools. In order to accommodate this desire for parental involvement, many schools have created parent–teacher bodies and have brought parents onto the school's board of governors. These moves have gone some way towards giving parents a role in the schools, but there is more that could be achieved.

---

*Introduction structure*

| Structure | Contains | Sentence |
|---|---|---|
| Situation | The topic and background | |
| Problem | The nature of the problem | |
| Solution | The solution | |
| Evaluation | How well the solution works | |

**TASK 8** *Reordering an introduction based on the S-P-S-E structure*

Reorder these sentences to provide an introduction to a paper entitled, 'Bridging the Gap between Testing and Technology in Schools'. The first sentence has been found for you.

| 1 | The need to improve education in the U.S. has received unprecedented attention recently in the media and in national and state elections. |
|---|---|
| ... | The technology prescription proposal holds that placing modern technology into schools will improve teaching and learning and will prepare students for an increasingly technological workplace. |
| ... | The situation is analogous to testing the accounting skills of modern accountants, but restricting them to using their fingers for calculations. |
| ... | The second prescription, which is often called high stakes testing, holds that standards- based accountability for students, teachers and schools will provide real incentives for improvements in teaching and learning. |
| ... | Recent research shows that paper-based written tests severely underestimate the performance of students used to working on computer (Russell, 1999; Russell & Haney, 1997). |
| ... | Prescriptions for improving schools have been many, but two of the most common are what might be called the technology and testing remedies. |
| ... | What is little recognized, however, is that these two strategies are working against each other because they fail to take the rise of technology into account. |

[Adapted slightly from: Russell M. & W. Haney. Bridging the Gap between Testing and Technology in Schools. *Education Policy Analysis Archives.* Volume 8 Number 19 http://epaa.asu.edu/epaa/v8n19.html]

**TASK 9** *Writing an introduction using the S-P-S-E structure*

Look at the notes you wrote for Task 6. Use your notes selectively to write a one-paragraph introduction with a Situation-Problem-Solution-Evaluation to an essay on that topic. You will have the opportunity to develop this writing later in the Unit.

# The language of coherence and connection

TASK 10 *Ensuring a coherent text: recognising the role of repetition and meaning relatedness*

A text is *coherent* when the ideas, sentences and details fit together in a way that helps readers follow the writer's train of thought. The underlined words in the text below all help to ensure a coherent development of the writer's ideas. Key terms are repeated throughout a text and are related to a number of other terms. *Girls* is a key term in the text below (mentioned 5 times) and is clearly related to other terms such as *females/boys/gender/children/them*.

Put each of the <u>underlined</u> words under one of the headings in the table (below) following the examples given.

| Repetition of key terms | Meaning-related expressions |
|---|---|
| girls | females/boys/gender/children/them |
| education | school/primary school/school fees |
|  |  |
|  |  |
|  |  |
|  |  |
|  |  |

The latest <u>UN report</u> on <u>education</u> says <u>girls</u> face sharp discrimination in access to <u>education</u>, which means millions of <u>them</u> are prevented from attending <u>school</u>. In addition, the <u>report</u> says the lack of <u>gender equality</u> in <u>education</u> is an important obstacle to social and economic progress.

In many developing countries, particularly in South Asia and sub-Saharan Africa, there are only seven <u>girls</u> in <u>primary school</u> for every 10 <u>boys</u>. In the world's two most populous countries, India and China, <u>boys</u> continue to outnumber <u>girls</u> in <u>schools</u>. The annual *Education for All* <u>report</u> by <u>UNESCO</u> says the proportion of <u>girls</u> in <u>school</u> did rise slightly in the past decade. Nevertheless more than half of the 104 million <u>children</u> out of <u>school</u> are still <u>females</u>, making <u>gender parity</u> in <u>education</u> a distant goal in more than 50 countries. The <u>UN</u> says that in many countries, high <u>school fees</u>, early marriage, and economic pressure to put <u>children</u> to work early block girls from school.

**TASK 11** *Recognising coherence strategies in a text*

In Unit 6, Task 7, we used the following table to show you the strategies writers use to link sentences together to form texts. These strategies are ways of making a text coherent.

Find examples of **four** strategies from the text in Task 10 (above). Strategy 2 has been completed for you as an example.

| Coherence strategy | Examples |
|---|---|
| 1 Repeating a word or words from a sentence in the following sentence. | |
| 2 Use a synonym (word with same meaning) of a word from a sentence in the following one. | *prevented from – block* |
| 3 Use a pro-form (e.g. pronoun) in the following sentence. | |
| 4 Use a sequence marker [e.g. Firstly, secondly/a), b), c)]. | |
| 5 Repeat a sentence structure. | |
| 6 Use connectives (e.g. moreover, firstly, etc.). | |
| 7 Use a hyponym (e.g. police station → building/car → means of transport). | |

**TASK 12** *Making a text coherent by supplying pro-forms and synonyms*

Complete each of the gaps in the following text by inserting *either*:

a) a pronoun

   *or*

b) a nominalised form of a verb (synonym) from the preceding sentence.

The first two are done for you as an example.

Many people assume that democracy is a naturally developing system, and still more assume that (1) _____*it*_____ has always existed in the United States. This (2) _____*assumption*_____ is wrong because, as the excerpt below indicates, developing democracy in the United States has been a decidedly difficult and sometimes very contentious matter. The (3) _____ of democracy is

an argumentative process, one that requires both time and patience.
(4) _____ who assumed that the newly emerging nations growing out of the breakup of the Soviet Union in 1990–91 would turn to democracy would need to re-examine the history of the United States, or England, or France (or any of the democratic nations of today).
A (5) _____ would show that the move to democratize Eastern Europe and Central Asia is just starting and that (6) _____ a movement will require nurturing and encouragement from all sources. Democracy is a difficult system both to institute and to maintain.

[Extracted from http://www.globaled.org/issues/177.pdf page 3]

## Connecting ideas in a text

Strategy 6 from the coherence table in Task 11 concerns the use of connectives. Table 9.1 (below) lists the most common connectives.

*Table 9.1 The most common connectives*

| To signal a: | Connectives | | |
|---|---|---|---|
| reinforcement of ideas | for example<br>also | in addition<br>furthermore | moreover<br>more importantly |
| change of ideas | however<br>but<br>instead<br>in contrast | on the other hand<br>although | yet<br>nevertheless<br>in spite of |
| conclusion | in conclusion<br>thus | accordingly<br>therefore | finally |

**TASK 13** *Exploring how ideas fit together to form a coherent text*
You have already read the text below. Read it again and think about how the sentences/ideas relate to each other.

Notice that some sentences have a number in brackets before them. These numbers correspond to the questions that follow the text. Choose the best answer from the options for each numbered sentence. The first one is done for you (on page 131).

> (1) It is well known that girls face sharp discrimination in access to education, which means millions of them are prevented from going to school. (2) Furthermore, the lack of gender equality in education is an important obstacle to social and economic progress.

(3) In many developing countries, particularly in South Asia and sub-Saharan Africa, there are only seven girls in primary school for every 10 boys. (4) In the world's two most populous countries, India and China, boys continue to outnumber girls in schools. (5) The annual *Education for All* report by UNESCO says the proportion of girls in school did rise slightly in the past decade. (6) Nevertheless more than half of the 104 million children out of school are still females, making gender parity in education a distant goal in more than 50 countries. (7) The UN says that in many countries, high school fees, early marriage, and economic pressure to put children to work early block girls from school.

(8) Christopher Colclough, the Paris-based director for the *Education for All* report, is calling for a change in the cultural and social values that keep girls out of school, particularly in poor countries.

(9) "The poor countries in the world tend to be the ones in which the social norms and values of society are most tolerant of inequality, and where the roles of men and women in society are more sharply different," he said. "Parents give different opportunities and different resources to boys and girls stemming from those different values."

(10) The United Nations is calling for countries to make primary education free, and reduce the dependence of poor households on child labor to ensure that more girls get into school. (11) It says educating girls has a high payoff by increasing household incomes and reducing poverty. (12) Mr. Colclough also is asking countries to adopt innovative methods to help girls stay in school. (13) He cites the example of one of the world's poorest countries, Bangladesh, where several programs have helped tens-of-thousands of poor girls reach secondary school.

(14) "It is being done both by very imaginative approaches to school expansion, which have emphasized the role of women teachers, emphasized flexibility in terms of the school timetable, and also by the introduction of scholarships … which have been focused on the poor," he said.

[Adapted from – http://www.voanews.com/article.cfm?objectID=545388A3-9A35-498C-9CCBF8AAF5D7789A# visited 07/11/03]

1 a) definition
  b) classification
  c) <u>introducing the situation</u>

2 a) reinforcing the situation
  b) contrasting with situation
  c) introducing a problem

3 a) comparison
  b) example of the situation
  c) contrast

4 a) reinforcement
  b) classification
  c) definition

5 a) comparison
  b) a change in the situation
  c) further example of the situation

6 a) support for the original situation
  b) reinforcement of the change
  c) comparison with 50 countries

7 a) the problem defined
  b) reinforcing the situation
  c) classification

8 a) recommendation
  b) definition
  c) example

9 a) explanation of problem
  b) classification
  c) result

10 a) example
   b) recommendation
   c) contrast

11 a) making a contrast
   b) giving a reason
   c) showing a cause

12 a) reinforcement
   b) request
   c) opinion

13 a) evidence for recommendation
   b) recommendation
   c) contrast

14 a) details
   b) comparison
   c) definition

## Process writing: Teacher evaluation

**TASK 14** *Looking at how a teacher evaluates work*
Thus far in this course we have asked you to evaluate your own writing and also encouraged you to get your peers to give you feedback on your writing. The next step is teacher evaluation. It is vitally important that you are aware of how your teacher will evaluate your writing.

On page 132–3 is a set of marking criteria and a set of comments from teachers at an educational institution. Your task is to match the teacher's comments to the criteria they have been using. The first one is done for you as an example.

1 __D__   2 _____   3 _____   4 _____   5 _____
6 _____   7 _____   8 _____   9 _____

| Content criteria | Teacher's comments |
|---|---|
| 1 Introduction which highlights the question and establishes the writer's point of view (thesis/argument) | A Students should show that they understand the ideas that they are discussing. It is not enough just to define the concepts; they should be able to evaluate them as well. |
| 2 Well organised with a clear overall progression of ideas | B Students need to show that they have thought about the ideas they are discussing and are not merely repeating what they heard in a lecture or read in a book. |
| 3 Demonstrates clear understanding of concepts | C Any claim that is made needs to be supported by examples and other relevant evidence. The sources of the evidence must be academically reliable. |
| 4 Evidence of critical thinking about theories and ideas discussed in the essay | D This shows that the student is dealing with the topic in the essay title and tells the reader how the topic is to be answered. |
| 5 Provides adequate and relevant support for claims that are made | E This is the last chance the writer has to impress the reader. This section should restate the writer's strongest arguments in support of her claim. |
| 6 The main points are made | F The essay should have an appropriate paragraph structure with clear and precise sentences that develop the arguments in a coherent and logical |

## Writing criteria

| | |
|---|---|
| 7 Arguments are carefully constructed | G The reader should be clearly able to follow the argument without getting confused and having to go back and read it all again. |
| 8 Accurate in terms of grammatical usage, appropriateness of vocabulary, and spelling | H Students often fail to follow the referencing system asked for by their departments. They do not seem to think it is important how references are written. |

## Research

| | |
|---|---|
| 9 Use up-to-date research sources, correctly referenced using a bibliographical system approved by your teachers | I It is amazing how many students do not proof-read their essays before handing them in. Inaccurate grammar and spelling makes it very difficult to read and so the writer loses marks. |

**TASK 15** *Establishing the teacher's evaluation criteria*

In groups, discuss how the criteria listed in Task 14 compare with the criteria used in your institution. Prepare some questions to ask your teacher about the criteria she or he uses for evaluating writing. Remember to ask whether the teacher uses the same criteria for giving feedback during teaching as for making evaluations of writing that is 'finished'. Make sure you completely understand the criteria that will be used for evaluating your writing for Task 16, and for your writing in the last unit of this course (Unit 10).

**TASK 16** *Writing a text using the S-P-S-E structure*

Look again at the Introduction you wrote for Task 9. Use this text (or a revision of it) as the introduction to an essay which develops the generalisations you made (in your introduction) into a complete essay.

# UNIT 10 Creating the whole text

This unit aims to improve your writing skills by:

1. putting together everything you have been learning and practising
2. showing how to write a short and fairly simple report of a survey
3. practising writing an academic paper on a topic you are interested in.

## Structure of the research report or paper

The most common structure of a research report, a thesis or a research article is referred to as IMRD, which stands for Introduction, Method, Results and Discussion. In the social sciences especially, the literature review is considered so important that (rather than being part of the Introduction) it is given a section to itself. Look at the summary below.

*Key features of each aspect of a research paper structure*

**Introduction**
Mapping of the field (in some disciplines, there will also be a literature review)
Identifying a research 'gap'
Making a claim about needed research
Giving some idea of the MRD approach that will be used

**Method**
Answering: How will this research be done? With what materials or subjects? How many? etc.
Working according to the principles of Clarity and Reality
Using the Relevance principle to dictate the amount of detail to use

**Results**
Answering: What happened? Why? How sure can I be of the meaning of these results?
Working according to the principles of Honesty and Reality

**Discussion**
This is probably the single most important part of the report, since it is here that you demonstrate that you understand and can interpret what you have done.

**TASK 1** *Recognising the structure of a research paper*

Read the research article (below) entitled *Free online availability substantially increases a paper's impact* by Steve Lawrence, NEC Research Institute, Princeton, NJ, USA, lawrence@research.nj.nec.com. See whether you can find paragraphs of the text that generally deal with each of the key IMRD areas. Circle either I, M, R, or D for each of the paragraphs.

| Para | Key area | Para | Key area | Para | Key area |
|------|----------|------|----------|------|----------|
| 1 | I M R D | 2 | I M R D | 3 | I M R D |
| 4 | I M R D | 5 | I M R D | 6 | I M R D |
| 7 | I M R D | 8 | I M R D | | |

1  The volume of scientific literature far exceeds the ability of scientists to identify and use all relevant information. The ability to locate relevant research quickly will dramatically improve communication and scientific progress. Although availability varies greatly by discipline, more than a million research articles are now freely available on the web.

2  Here we investigate the impact of free online availability by analysing citation rates. Online availability of an article may not greatly improve access and impact without efficient and comprehensive search services; a substantial percentage of the literature needs to be indexed by these search services before scientists consider them useful. In computer science, a substantial percentage of the literature is online and available through search engines such as Google, or specialized services such as ResearchIndex – although the greatest impact of online availability is yet to come, because comprehensive search services and more powerful search methods have become available only recently.

3  We analysed 119,924 conference articles in computer science and related disciplines, obtained from DBLP (dblp.uni-trier.de). In these fields, conference articles are typically formal publications and are often more prestigious than journal articles, with acceptance rates at some conferences below 10%. We estimated citation counts and online availability using ResearchIndex, excluding self-citations.

4  Figure 1 shows the probability that an article is freely available online as a function of the number of citations to the article, and the year of publication of the article. The results are dramatic, showing a clear correlation between the number of times an article is cited and the probability that the article is online. More highly cited articles, and more recent articles, are significantly more likely to be online, in computer science. The mean number of citations to offline articles is 2.74, and the mean number of citations to online articles is 7.03, an increase of 157%.

5　We analysed differences within publication venues (the proceedings of a conference for a particular year, for example), looking at the percentage increase in citation rates for online articles. When offline articles were more highly cited, we used the negative of the percentage increase for offline articles: hence if the average number of citations for offline articles is two, and the average for online articles is four, the percentage increase would be 100%. For the opposite situation, the percentage increase would be −100%.

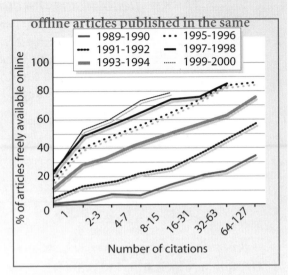

Figure 1: Analysis of 119,924 conference articles in computer science and related disciplines.
The actual percentage of articles available online is greater, owing to limitations in the extraction of article information from online documents and limitations in locating articles on the web. Only points with greater than 100 articles are computed.

6　Averaging the percentage increase across 1,494 venues containing at least five offline and five online articles results in an average of 336% (median 158%) more citations to online computer-science articles compared with offline articles published in the same venue (see Figure 2).

The graph shows the distribution of the percentage increase for the average number of citations to online articles compared to offline articles. The analysis covers 1,494 publication venues containing at least 5 online and 5 offline articles. For 90% of venues, online articles are more highly cited on average. On average there are 336% more citations to online articles compared to venue [the first, second (median), and third quartiles of the distribution are 58%, 158%, and 361%].

7　If we assume that articles published in the same venue are of similar quality, then the analysis by venue suggests that online articles are more highly cited because of their easier availability. This assumption is likely to be more valid for

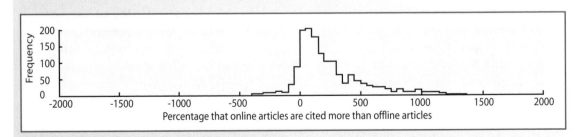

Figure 2: Analysis of citation rates within publication venues.

top-tier conferences with very high acceptance standards. Restricting our analysis to the top 20 publication venues by average citation rate gives an increase of 286% (median 284%) in the citation rate for online articles.

8 Free online availability facilitates access in many ways, including provision of online archives; direct connections among scientists or research groups; hassle-free links from e-mail, discussion groups and other services; indexing by web search engines; and the creation of third-party search services. Free online availability of scientific literature offers substantial benefits to science and society. To maximize impact, minimize redundancy and speed scientific progress, authors and publishers should aim to make research easy to access.

http://www.nature.com/nature/debates/e-access/Articles/lawrence.html 09/09/05

## Creating your own research

In this section you will go through the research steps on a very small scale, to allow you to practise creating and writing about some research of your own. The following task asks you to carry out a small amount of questionnaire data collection (that is, research) on a specific topic. Your teacher might choose a different topic, especially if a lot of students in the class have a similar interest; alternatively, if you are working by yourself, you can replace the topic with one of your own.

**TASK 2** *The Method section and data collection*

You are going to learn more about other people's attitudes towards, and knowledge of, the importance of preserving biodiversity. You will do this by collecting questionnaire data; you need to collect responses from at least 12 people (this is not statistically analysable but will give you enough raw material to work with for this exercise).

In groups of three, devise a questionnaire to find out your class's views (or those of some other group as instructed by your teacher) on preserving biodiversity.

Remember that when you write the Methods section, you will need to provide enough information for another researcher to repeat the experiment, so work carefully. Refer back to Unit 7 to re-read about the Reality Principle and try to ask realistic, answerable questions; also look at Unit 7 for more ideas on writing the Methods section.

Here are some example questions: add more of your own or improve on these.

- Are you aware of the word 'biodiversity'?                $(+)\ 5\ 4\ 3\ 2\ 1\ (-)$
- How important is preserving biodiversity
  in today's world?                                        $(+)\ 5\ 4\ 3\ 2\ 1\ (-)$
- Would you give up your job if that helped
  preserve biodiversity?                                   $(+)\ 5\ 4\ 3\ 2\ 1\ (-)$
- Is it possible to develop economically and
  preserve biodiversity?                                   $(+)\ 5\ 4\ 3\ 2\ 1\ (-)$

When the questionnaire is ready, give it to as many people as you can – at least 12.

**TASK 3** *Analysing the results*

When your group has collected all the data, tabulate the results to show how your respondents answered the questionnaire. Here is an example of what the table might start to look like as you enter the responses.

| Aware? | | | | | Important? | | | | |
|---|---|---|---|---|---|---|---|---|---|
| 5 | 4 | 3 | 2 | 1 | 5 | 4 | 3 | 2 | 1 |
| // | / | /// | / | / | //// | / | | | |
| | | | | | | | | | |
| | | | | | | | | | |
| | | | | | | | | | |
| | | | | | | | | | |
| | | | | | | | | | |
| | | | | | | | | | |
| | | | | | | | | | |
| | | | | | | | | | |
| | | | | | | | | | |
| | | | | | | | | | |

Remember that, as you learned in Unit 8, in a research essay, report or academic paper, the Results section **describes but does not interpret** your results.

Write the Results section factually and simply, keeping in mind the *R=R* from Unit 8: Results = Reporting. You are going to need the Clarity and Honesty Principles here!

## TASK 4  *Discussing the results*

What do these results **tell** you? Did everyone agree? If not, was it 50:50, or more mixed? Was the pattern of opinions different on different questions? If so, why might that be? Ask yourself questions that try to dig into what the tabulated results might suggest about this group of people's beliefs and values about biodiversity. Remember that on a tiny sample like this, you cannot generalise; you can only interpret meaning within this group itself. (When you begin real empirical research in content areas you will take whole classes in Research Methods.) Look back at Unit 8 to remind yourself of what you learned about the Relevance Principle; that, along with the Honesty Principle, is very important in writing a Discussion section.

The skills of peer work that you have learned during this course will be very helpful now you are working on your own whole study and report. Discuss with classmates, with another group of students, or even with one or two friends, what your results could be said to be telling you. Listen carefully to their questions and interests and respond to them as you plan and draft the next stage (Task 5).

## TASK 5  *Writing up your research*

When you are quite clear on the meaning of your results, write a report on your findings under the IMRD headings:
- Introduction
- Methodology
- Results
- Discussion.

This is the simplest organisation for writing about academic work you have done. It certainly does not cover every kind of academic writing you will do, but it is a very useful structure to master, and then to adapt for your own more advanced academic writing needs.

Your teacher will read and mark your report using the criteria you became familiar with in Unit 7: clarity, organisation, vocabulary, and language (grammar, spelling and punctuation), and also the very important criterion of 'Ideas'. Make sure you fully understand what your teacher is looking for when marking for 'ideas'. Refer to Appendix B to help you get a sense of what to aim for. Also remember about 'fulfilling the task' – achieving what the task has asked of you and what your teacher (or your other, real-life audience) expects.

# Plagiarism ... and how to avoid it

> *Plagiarism is a form of intellectual dishonesty or theft. When a person plagiarises s/he 'steals' someone else's words or ideas by passing them off as their own.*

Read the sentence above again: it is important; it is true. But there is a problem.

The problem is, we took that sentence from a published booklet about plagiarism, and [so far] we have failed to acknowledge it.

## What must you acknowledge?

You must acknowledge every direct quotation you use from someone else's words that you have seen written down (in a book, journal article, newspaper, on the web, etc.). You probably knew that already. But what is harder is figuring out when to acknowledge the influence of other people's words on you when you are not directly quoting them.

**TASK 6** *What constitutes plagiarism?*
Which of these is plagiarism?

The list on the next page describes five situations where someone else's (or several people's) words are used; use ✓ if you think this is OK to do or ✗ if you think it would be plagiarism.

| 1 | Direct duplication by taking material from a book or website, etc. and making people think you wrote that material | |
|---|---|---|
| 2 | Copying another's work, for example, another student's assignment, and making people think you did it yourself | |
| 3 | Using parts of several other people's work and joining them together, then making people think you did it yourself | |
| 4 | Rewriting another's work using many of your own words, but keeping the other writer's meaning, important parts of the ideas in their words, and keeping their organisation of ideas and points – and making people think this is your own work | |
| 5 | Handing in work that you have done with a group of peers without acknowledging that it is not your individual work | |

The sentence displayed at the start of this section is an example of plagiarism! Why? Because this sentence was found in someone else's text and we used it without acknowledging it. It is taken from a little leaflet called 'Plagiarism: and how to avoid it' published by the Language and Learning Skills Unit at the University of Melbourne in Australia. The leaflet is based on material that is part of the University's 'Policy on Academic Honesty and Plagiarism', which can be found online at: www.services.unimelb.edu.au/llsu/

All of the cases above (1–5) are examples of plagiarism. In many cultures it is not only permissible to directly use other people's words, it is considered skilful. The Chinese love to use the sayings of Confucius and other respected scholars. In Arab culture, until recently the main mode of learning was through memorisation and imitation of criterion texts. Consequently, plagiarism was not always recognised as such; it was often seen as an aspect of learning.

## How do you avoid plagiarism?

### Quotations: respecting the words of others

Quotations are mainly used in writing to provide support for the writer's argument; to give examples of different viewpoints on a topic; or to highlight a position you will go on to disagree with. Quotations rarely prove or disprove a point. Instead, they are used by the author of this text to 'suggest' or 'indicate' a relationship between her or his own research or evidence or argument, and that of another person – usually a recognised authority on this topic.

If quotations are to fulfil their function they need to be identical to the original, word for word, and must be attributed to the author. There are three main ways of integrating quotations into your text. Each is listed below, followed by an example.

1 Quotations that consist of a phrase or a clause must be contained within a sentence.

> Alderson and Wall (1993) pointed out that the existence of washback – the influence of a test on teaching and learning – has seldom been demonstrated or supported with empirical evidence. Furthermore, they suggested that 'the quality of washback might be independent of the quality of the test' (118).

2 If the quotation consists of one or more complete sentences, it an follow a colon and requires quotation marks.

> Hamp-Lyons, Chen and Mok (2002) found that helping students learn how to write well in their second language is no easy task: 'Teachers' comments that concentrate on lower order problems, such as spelling and grammar, and teachers' feedback that aims at eradicating student errors have been notably unsuccessful in helping students to improve either their language accuracy or the substance of their writing in subsequent written work.' (2)

3 Longer quotations (more than 60 words or 5 lines) need to be 'set off' from your text (that is, treated differently) for example indented. Quotation marks are not needed. Look at the example below.

> The dilemma of choice between principles and practice is a difficult one. Hamp-Lyons (1999) argues that:
>
> > Standards of conduct and codes of ethics hold great importance, and yet they do not supersede individual conscience. But ultimately, each person will make a personal choice based on their knowledge, experience, values, constraints, priorities. The dialogue with respected professional peers provides vital support to that decision-making, but in the end it is the individual's responsibility. (590)

**TASK 7** *Using and commenting on quotes*

In quoting another person's words, you are effectively allowing them to speak in the middle of your own words. It can be confusing for a reader to figure out how you are using the quotation – whether you agree or disagree with it and how strongly. Fortunately, there are a set of useful verbs for indicating this to your reader. They are:

| | | |
|---|---|---|
| *suggests* | *indicates* | *implies* |
| *shows* | *illustrates* | *tells us* |
| *supports* | *lends weight to* | *argues* |

Revise the underlined sentence in the text below in the light of the Honesty principle. [Note: The underlined sentence only relates to the text in the extract.]

When discussing the role of feedback on non-native students' writing, Ferris (2006) recommends 'peer feedback sessions which are "teacher-choreographed"– including careful modeling and training of students prior to beginning peer feedback activities, providing specific tasks and questions for peer feedback sessions' (17). Matsuda (1999) says that 'Invention strategies, multiple drafts and formative feedback – both by the teacher and by peers ... become important parts of writing instruction in many L2 writing classrooms.' Hamp-Lyons et al (2002) say 'Students reported that they considered teacher feedback given to their work both during and after the writing process important.' <u>Most studies have found that students prefer teacher feedback over peer feedback.</u>

## Creating citations

In-text citations such as those we have dealt with above need to be fully identified in the *References* or *Works Cited* lists at the end of a text. These list all the sources used in a text and are arranged alphabetically by author's last name or, when there is no author, by the first word of the title but not *A*, *An* or *The*. Within the list, if an author is cited more than once, then the author's entries are ordered chronologically by date (with most recent first). There are numerous internationally recognised systems for identifying sources, such as the Modern Languages Association (MLA). The basic MLA format for an entry is:

Author(s) [family name & personal name in full] <u>Title of Book</u>. City of Publication: Publisher, Year of publication.

Author(s) [family name & personal name in full] "Title of Article." <u>Title of Periodical</u> Vol (Year): pages.

You will need to find out which system is in use in your institution and learn how to use it.

······················

**TASK 8**   *Using the MLA system for references/cited works*
Create an alphabetically arranged Works Cited list from these
sources using the MLA example given above. The references have
become mixed up and need to be rearranged.

Hamp-Lyons, Liz "Social, professional and individual responsibility
in language testing." System, 28 (2000): 579–591.

Ferris, D. "Responding to writing." In K. Hyland & F. Hyland.
Feedback in Second Language Writing: Contexts and Issues. New
York: Cambridge University Press, 2006.

Alderson, J.C. & D. Wall. "Does washback exist?" Applied Linguistics
14, 2 (1993): 115–129.

Matsuda, P. "Second language writing in the twentieth century: A
situated historical perspective." In B. Kroll (Ed.) Exploring the
Dynamics of Second Language Writing. New York: Cambridge
University Press, 2003.

Hamp-Lyons, L., J. Chen & J. Mok. "Supporting secondary English
language teachers and learners: Developing good teaching
strategies for giving written feedback on student work; and good
learning strategies for effective use of teacher feedback." Report to
the Standing Committee of Language Education and Research
(SCOLAR) Hong Kong: SAR, 2002.

*Using the APA system for references/cited works*
Another popular international system for identifying sources is
**TASK 9**   the American Psychological Association (APA) system. Its basic
format is:

**Author(s) family name + initials. (Year of publication).** *Title of
Book: Capital letter also for subtitle.* **City of Publication:
Publisher.**

**Author(s) family name + initials. (Year of publication).** Title of
Article. *Title of Periodical, volume number,* **pages.**

For example:

Lockhart, C. & Ng, P. (1995). Analyzing talk in peer response groups:
Stances, functions, and content. *Language Learning, 45,* 605–655.

Create an alphabetically arranged Works Cited list from the sources
in Task 8 and the one above, using the APA system.

**TASK 10** *Comparing MLA and APA systems*

With a partner decide:

a) on the main differences between the two systems, and

b) which system you prefer.

# In your own words: Paraphrase and summary

In the English language-using academic world it is vital that your thinking is your own, and that it is represented in your own words supported by reference to the words of others. In the section above we have shown you how to quote and how to use citations to integrate other people's text into your own text. However, it is not always possible to use quotations; you may not be able to find an appropriate quotation, or it may be too lengthy to integrate. At times like this you will use the skills of **paraphrase** and **summary**.

Paraphrase involves putting someone else's text into your own words. We usually only paraphrase parts of a text: if you think you need to paraphrase a whole text, there is something wrong, because it means you are not using your own ideas and making your own points. Go back and think again about what you know about your subject. However well you paraphrase someone else's words, it is still important that you give credit to them for their ideas. You still need to make a citation to them.

**TASK 11** *Paraphrasing without plagiarising*

Read the original paragraph below and decide which paraphrase (1 to 3) is acceptable, that is, does not in any way plagiarise the source.

## Being old in the global village

In later life the saying 'no man is an island' becomes truer than ever. Older men and women rely on collective support and this can be divided into three overlapping systems. The first is economic, broadly interpreted to include paid and unpaid work. Wherever pensions are low, restricted to civil servants and the military, or non-existent, work is the main means of support in later life. Some elders, usually men, are able to continue in paid jobs, especially if they can shift to easier work, but most are likely to be doing unpaid work such as farming, childcare or housework – often filling in for family members who work in the formal economy.

http://www.healthmatters.org.uk/stories/wilson.html#

**Paraphrase 1**

When we get older the saying 'no man is an island' becomes truer than ever. Middle-aged men and women rely on collective support and this support can be divided into three overlapping systems. The first is financial, broadly interpreted to include paid and unpaid work. Wherever pensions are low, restricted to civil servants and the military, or not available, work is the major means of support in later life. Some older people, usually men, are able to continue in paid jobs, especially if they can change to easier work, but most are likely to be doing unpaid work such as farming, childcare or housework – often substituting for family members who work in the formal economy.

**Paraphrase 2**

There are three support systems available for older people. Employment, paid or unpaid, is the major means of support particularly in situations where pensions are inadequate, available only to certain groups or not available at all. Some older people, most commonly men, engage in paid employment, usually in easier jobs while most older people undertake unpaid work in agriculture, childcare or housework. This latter group often take the place of family who are employed elsewhere.

**Paraphrase 3**

According to Wilson, older people rely on 'three overlapping systems' of 'collective support'. The main support is through work whether paid or unpaid. Not surprisingly when pensions are inadequate, only available to certain economic groups, or not available at all, work is the main provider for older people. Some senior citizens, invariably men, undertake remunerative employments, usually changing to less demanding jobs, while most engage in unpaid work in agriculture, minding children, or doing domestic chores. This latter group are 'often filling in for family members who work in the formal economy'.

## In your own words: Summary

A **summary** is a short and selective version of another text's main ideas. Summaries are substantially shorter than the original and take a broad overview of the text. It is necessary to attribute summarised materials with an in-text citation.

When summarising, it is useful to read the complete text and underline/highlight the main ideas, then to summarise in your own words the key main idea of the text.

**TASK 12** *Summarising*

Read this abbreviated paper by Paul Christ. Summarise it in your own words. Use about 200 words.

# Is the Internet Undermining Customer Value?

The Internet's dramatic impact on business operations is causing some to conclude that business success may be hard to sustain. In particular, the speed at which information is exchanged and knowledge is gained makes competitive advantage a fleeting proposition – here today, gone tomorrow. While this picture of business is somewhat dire, most executives and business owners are probably not losing much sleep over what these prognosticators envision. But maybe they should, especially when it comes to creating and maintaining customer value.

## The Essence of Value

From a customer's perspective, value is the perception of benefits received for what he/she must give up. In other words, what you get for your money. For some products there are tangible aspects to value obtained in a purchase. For instance, you receive three donuts from one store for the same amount that another store will sell you two. Yet this type of value essentially amounts to a pricing battle that is very tricky to maintain, so many companies find that a better way to create value is to build perceptual value. That is, get the customer to "think" there is a difference rather than have the customer actually "know" there is a difference. Whether a company chooses to focus on the tangible or the perceptual (or both) for creating and maintaining

customer value, it can be argued that the Internet has made this job much more difficult. For tangible value, the Internet is the perfect venue for supporting a price war. The Internet closely represents a state of pure competition (an economics term), where there exists many buyers and sellers and a lot of market information on which to base decisions. In fact, with the proliferation of Internet acquisition tools, such as online auctions and shopping robot software, it will be very difficult for any company's product to sustain value based solely on a low price position.

With value through price advantage being problematic, companies must then move to build value in perceptual ways. But here again the Internet may present problems. Here are a few examples:

### Reliability

The perception a product is more reliable than another might add value since it is associated with fewer usage problems. In other words, it saves on frustration. Yet the Internet may knock this down. A product's reliability can be explained by the company using research information such as test results, but many customers want to see real customers experiencing it before they make a judgment of reliability. For example, auto buyers have learned to take an automaker's claim of reliability with a grain of salt and instead have relied more on Internet chat rooms, forums and usenet groups, which open customers to potentially thousands of opinions. More than likely not all opinions are good and may lead to perceived reliability estimates that are well below the company's research forecast.

## Overall Cost Savings

Value can be obtained if the user of a product feels she is saving in some other ways. For example, the time it takes to learn how to use one product may be shorter than the time a user must invest to learn how to use another product. Added costs may also occur if the product does not match with other products the users own and, consequently, requires the users to unexpectedly purchase additional new products to go along with a new purchase. This was a big complaint with Windows XP, where users were often forced to make upgrade purchases because favorite applications did not run under the new operating system. Yet, once again the Internet may narrow this value gap by

providing access to extensive tutorials and how-to instructional guides that may show the competitor's product is not hard to learn or that a competitor's product works with existing products.

The Internet may not shake out value from all products but for many it will. Reduced value means the company's product is not as attractive as it once was, which means the company has two options: reduce price or maintain price but add new value propositions. Both options are worth exploring but, as was noted above, pricing wars are difficult to sustain and consequently are only a short-run solution. To really add value requires constantly evaluating new value propositions. Sources for new value propositions include research and development activity, asking customers, doing competitive analysis, and, of course, using the Internet for research. Adding value is a difficult, time-consuming undertaking but necessary in the Internet age.

To read the complete article, go to: http://www.knowthis.com/articles/marketing/customervalue.htm

# 'Authorial identity' – sounding like your academic self

Effective academic writers manage to sound like real people even when they are discussing very complex ideas and data in a very serious book or journal article.

**TASK 13** *The voice of the writer*
Read Extracts A and B and discuss with a partner or friend what makes them 'alive'. Why do they sound as though a real person wrote them?

1 Extract **A** is from the literature review section of an article about the consequences of high-stakes tests. (High-stakes tests are tests that have a big influence on a person's future, for example, one that allows someone to 'graduate' from high school or get a university place.) We used this text in Unit 5. If you are interested in high-stakes tests, you can find the full article at: http://www.pop.psu.edu/general/pubs/working_papers/psu-pri/wp0301.pdf (12-12-03). The full reference is: Reardon, S.F. and C. Galindo, Do High-Stakes Tests Affect Students' Decisions to Drop Out of School? Evidence from NELS. Paper prepared for presentation at the Annual Meeting of the American Educational Research Association, New Orleans, LA, April 1–5, 2002.

a) In Extract A consider:
   i)   the effect of using more Active than Passive voice sentences.
   ii)  the use of Present Simple tense versus Past Simple tense.
   iii) the effect of the word 'puzzling' in the sentence 'The discrepancy between the Jacob (2001) ... results is puzzling, since both use the same data'.
   iv)  the absence of the personal pronoun 'we' (two authors).

b) What kind of overall stance do they take on the issues they discuss? Is it:
   — a scholarly approach?
   — a combative approach?

---

**Extract A**

Six years ago, when Reardon reviewed existing research, there was almost no empirical evidence regarding the effects of high-stakes testing on student motivation, achievement, and dropout patterns (Reardon 1996). In recent years, however, several analyses of survey data have been published. The evidence from these, however, is mixed.

The best quality evidence on the association between high-stakes testing and dropping out comes from two recent analyses of the relationship between high school graduation test requirements and school completion using NELS data (Jacob 2001; Warren and Edwards 2001). Although Jacob (2001) found no reading and math achievement differences associated with the presence of graduation tests, he found that dropout rates are roughly 6.5% greater among students in the bottom quintile on achievement tests in states with high school graduation test requirements than comparable students in states without such tests. Warren and Edwards (2001), however, find no effect of graduation tests on the probability of dropping out. Warren and Edwards, moreover, like Jacob, test for an interaction between the graduation test requirement and student achievement levels, in order to see if test policies disproportionately impact low-achieving students, but they find no interaction.

The discrepancy between the Jacob (2001) and Warren and Edwards (2001) results is puzzling, since both use the same data. There are some differences in the variables included in their models, but not dramatic ones. A close examination of the precise NELS sample they use, however, reveals a potential reason for the discrepancy. Warren and Edwards use school administrator reports about the presence of a graduation test requirement as their treatment variable. Jacob points out, however, that this data is missing for a number of students (971 of 12,171 students in his sample are missing this variable). Importantly, it is missing in most of these cases because these students had dropped out of school and so had no school administrator questionnaire in their record. Warren and Edwards find no effect of the tests on dropout rates, but that may be because they have excluded from their sample a large number of dropouts, who may have disproportionately dropped out of schools with graduation test requirements.

On balance then, neither Jacob's nor Warren and Edwards' results can be taken as definitive. It would be useful to reanalyze the NELS data using Jacob's sample and Warren and Edwards' models.

2  Extract **B** is from 'The Language Socialization Paradigm For SLA*: What's In It For You?' by Kevin R. Gregg.
   a) In Extract **B** we hear the voice of an author much more than in Extract **A**. How is this achieved? Consider:
      i)   the use of the personal pronouns 'we', 'she' and 'I'
      ii)  the proportion of Active to Passive voice sentences
      iii) why Karen Watson-Gegeo is given her full name while the others are referred to by surname only?
   b) What kind of overall stance does the writer take on the issues he discusses, is it:
      — a scholarly approach?
      — a combative approach?

* Second Language Acquisition (SLA) is a theoretical and experimental field of study which looks at, and seeks to understand, the phenomenon of language development, in this case the acquisition of second languages.

**Extract B**

Since C.P. Snow, in his Reith lectures of 1959 (see Snow, 1993) first described the "two cultures" of science and the humanities, the gap between them has, if anything, widened. Where Snow saw mutual isolation and ignorance, however, recent years have witnessed a number of gross misrepresentations of, and even attacks on, the scientific enterprise, from a number of intellectual quarters—self-styled "feminists", self-styled "Marxists", and, of course, postmodernists of various stripes (see, e.g., Gross & Levitt, 1994; Sagan, 1996; Sokal & Bricmont, 1998, for documentation). The field of SLA has not been spared: a look at the "applied linguistics" literature all too easily turns up misinterpretations of natural sciences and misguided attempts to apply them to SLA (Edge, 1993; Larsen-Freeman, 1997; Schumann, 1983), doubts about the value of controlling for variables (Block, 1996), reduction of empirical claims to metaphors (Lantolf, 1996; Schumann, 1983), mockery of empirical claims in SLA as "physics envy" (Lantolf, 1996), and denials of the possibility of achieving objective knowledge (Lantolf, 1996). Although the standpoints are various, one common thread unites these papers: a fundamental misunderstanding of what science, and in particular cognitive science, is about (see, e.g., Gregg et al., 1997; Gregg, 2000). One sort of critique of SLA research conducted within the framework of standard cognitive science comes from some of those concerned with social and political aspects of second language use and teaching (e.g., Firth & Wagner, 1997; Pennycook, 1990). A recent, wide-ranging, and ambitious critique of this sort comes from Karen Watson-Gegeo.

Watson-Gegeo (2001) tells us that we are "at the beginning of a paradigm shift in the human and social sciences" that is "fundamentally transforming second language acquisition (SLA) and educational theory and research" (p. 1). Watson-Gegeo is not very forthcoming as to the nature of either the old paradigm or the new one; and indeed, one of the problems with her paper is the absence of anything that could be called evidence. Still, based on what she sees as this emerging new paradigm, she is explicit in arguing that we need a new paradigm for SLA, what she calls the "language socialization paradigm". I propose to look at the new cognitive science as Watson-Gegeo conceives it, and at her proposals for SLA research. It will be seen that her account of the former is generally vacuous or irrelevant where it is not simply incorrect, while the latter show little promise for a productive research program for SLA.

http://www.hawaii.edu/sls/uhwpesl/20(2)/GreggKevin.doc

3 Extract **C** is from 'Social Capital, Literacy Ecologies And Lifelong Learning: The Importance of "Process" In Repositioning Literacy Debates' by Ian Falk & Jo Balatti.

a) Comment on the various meanings of the personal pronoun in this extract. Who does:
   i)   'we' refer to in line 1?
   ii)  'our' refer to in line 10?
   iii) 'our' refer to in Line 22?
   iv)  'we' refer to in Line 24?

b) Does the widespread use of the Active voice make the extract:
   i)   more/less lively?
   ii)  easier to follow/more difficult to follow?

**Extract C**

*It is therefore a mistaken dichotomy to wonder whether the unit of analysis of identity should be the community or the person. The focus must be on the process of their mutual constitution.*

(Wenger, 1998, p. 146)

## Literacy as (Inter) Action

From the earliest moments of our lives **we** are engaged in          1
interaction with our environment. We are not simply 'born'
any more than we are simply 'babies'. At birth we are both the
cause and effect of interplay between mother and midwife,
forceps, doctor, father, towelling, metal instruments, tables and
nursing staff. We interact with people and things. How do we
know what is food and what is not? What is cold and hot? What
makes us cry, laugh, hurt? We can only reach a definition of
ourselves by reference to other people and other things.
However, **our** gaze over the last century or more has been          10
more 'on the baby' than on the interaction between baby and
her environment.

As babies grow into children, the interactions become more
frequent and diverse. The contexts vary, people vary, places
and things are more varied. Kids go home and they go to
school. They play sport and they use the internet. They learn to
read and write, go to church, make love and war. In all cases,
they only achieve this as joint accomplishments with other
human and physical elements of their environment. Their
learning is a co-production, drawing upon human and physical
resources in the interaction.

> This paper began from **our** belief that we tend to nominalise 22
> 'literacy' rather than 'operationalise' it as learning. From the
> time **we** first heard the term 'multiliteracies' (New London 24
> Group, 1997) we were uneasy about it without really knowing
> why. Perhaps it is because it makes an already too-complex
> matter even more complex, and then nominalises it into a big
> and powerful entity.
>
> http://pandora.nla.gov.au/pan/20993/20040719/ctldec.ntu.edu.au/Issue%20
> 2%20final.pdf 16/09/05

**TASK 14** *Identifying with the extract writers*

Look back at Extracts **A**, **B** and **C**, and think about how you
responded to them. Developing academic writers usually play 'safe'
and don't show much of their own 'identity' in their writing; as
writers become more confident they often become more willing to
write like a real person and not just imitate the most conventional
rules and genres of academic style. Ask yourself which of the features
of authorial identity in these extracts you might feel comfortable
using yourself.

**TASK 15** *Researching a topic*

And finally … the task below is only for those of you who are
graduate students, or students doing an undergraduate Honours
course, or working with close support and feedback from a teacher.

Choose one of the topics given below or a different topic in
consultation with your teacher.

Suggested topics
- How media violence touches children.
  Does exposure to violent images in the media – television,
  movies, video games, and music lead to an increasing tolerance
  for violence by young people?
- Global warming – Myth or Reality?
  Is there compelling evidence for or against the existence of
  global warming?

**Suggested procedure**

1 Research the topic using resources available to you: an Internet search, encyclopaedias, specialist media journals and media textbooks.

2 Create a Research Gap. If you cannot find one you may be able to use the fact your topic has probably not been researched in your region/country before.

3 Decide on a Method of data collection. This could involve either:
   - in-depth interviews with a small number of informants or questionnaire data from a large number
   - a survey of existing research on your topic, presenting summaries in the Result section and a synthesis in the Discussion section
   - a case study of one or two results claimed for global warming or media violence (for example, the Columbine shootings in Denver, Colorado, USA could be a case study for media violence).

4 Collect and report your data.

5 Analyse your data and report your results (as always, we suggest discussion with others once you have your results.

6 Interpret and discuss your results.

7 Revise your paper, perhaps working with peers.

8 Submit your paper to your teacher for comments, assessment and advice.

**Finale**

We hope that in completing *Study Writing* you will feel more confident of your ability to produce academic writing to a high standard. Further improvements can be made by:
- continuing to reflect on your own writing
- asking peers to comment on your writing
- analysing examples of others' academic writing.

We wish you 'good writing'.

Liz Hamp-Lyons
Ben Heasley

# UNIT 1 Teaching notes and Key

The Introduction forms a sequence that encourages students to reflect on what the course will be about and what they need to attend to in order to succeed in it.

**Timing**: Working through this material will take 40 minutes to an hour, depending on how much discussion time is available.

The first activity generates input to the second. There are no 'correct' answers, only sensible or thoughtless ones; students' views and comments can be tested out against several of the input texts/material later in this unit. You and your students might find it interesting to answer these questions again at the end of the course and compare their answers with those from the beginning. We expect and hope that students will have more to say about **how** they write when they finish this course, and that they will realise that good writing takes times and several attempts!

The purposes of the first activity are twofold.

- First, to get the students thinking and speaking about some fundamental issues of different ways of writing that are going to underpin the whole course; the purpose is **not** to have them see all the issues about academic writing at this stage. These issues will recur throughout the book and there will be other discussion opportunities
- Second, as a **pre-writing** task that will help students to write a rough draft in Task 5.

## What is a rough draft?

As explained in the footnote on page 16, a rough draft is a first version of a piece of writing: it might be early thinking about a topic for an essay or report; or, **as in this case**, it might be an activity that leads students to think about a topic, an event or an issue, in order to talk clearly about it later. You will want to **use the material prepared in this task for** brainstorming, creating an in-class needs analysis, or as input to later tasks in this unit (for example, Task 8). You will probably **not** want to collect in these rough drafts. There is more material about process writing in each unit of the book, with accompanying Teaching notes and Key.

## Distinguishing between academic and personal styles of writing

Tasks 1–5 will take about an hour; Task 5 may be done for homework.

**TASK 1**  **A  Any three of:**

- complex sentence
- serious subject
- reference to academics, 'linguists' and 'Noam Chomsky of …'
- use of passive voice 'Linguists were and remain convinced by Noam Chomsky …'
- shows truth status of statement, '**seemingly** hardwired into the brain'.

**B  Any three of:**

- vague vocabulary, such as 'way', 'says' and 'a lot' – lack of precision
- directly addressing the reader, 'you' – conversational style
- simple sentence structure.

**TASK 2**  As stated earlier, some academic situations may permit a more informal style than other situations, but, on the whole, the following features signify formal or informal writing.

1  Informal – use of 'I'; and short form, 'couldn't'
2  Formal – use of passive voice, 'were completed'; use of precise vocabulary, 'initial'
3  Informal – use of 'I' and 'your'; short form 'I'd'
4  Informal – in an academic work we would expect some bibliographic references after 'some researchers'
5  Informal – use of 'me'; short forms; vague vocabulary, 'much sense'
6  Informal – use of short form, 'We'll'; vague
7  Formal – complex sentence
8  Formal – use of connector, 'In addition'; impersonal style i.e. 'the research attempts' rather than 'I' or 'we'

**TASK 3**  From most to least academic: B, D, C, A. (See Task 4 for the explanations.)

**TASK 4**  Depending on the level of the students, they can be rewarded for getting just one aspect of the explanation right, or can be expected to do more.

**B:** This is the most academic, having been taken from a research book on academic writing. It exhibits complex sentence structure with 'distant' verb forms such as present perfect (e.g. 'have led'); high-level vocabulary, such as 'reciprocal relationship' and 'complex cognitive and linguistic skills'; content that displays the outcome of serious thought; and nominalisation. Students may not understand this term 'nominalisation', so explain that academic writers frequently use the noun forms of verbs to help focus their work on concepts rather than specific actions (e.g. using 'development', 'application' and 'activation' rather than 'develop', 'apply' and 'activate'). Nominalisation will be looked at more thoroughly in Unit 7.

**D:** This is the second most academic, being taken from a research report. It exhibits complex sentences; references '(Kunii, 1994)'; academic vocabulary, 'effectively', 'capability' and 'disseminated'; passives, 'it has been claimed'; and discourse markers, 'With this in mind', 'The capability to' and 'To prepare our students for these endeavours'. Text D is more explicit than Text B because of its academic genre – it is a research report.

**C:** This is a mixture of formal and informal modes. It contains direct reference to the reader, 'your' and 'you'; but it also contains a passive, 'the reader is focused'; and is itself a long, complex sentence. The text was taken from an instruction manual.

**A:** This could be part of a speech, or an informal letter or e-mail. The style is didactic rather than academic. The use of a question-and-answer sequence suggests informality, as does the use of the filler 'Anyway'.

**TASK 5**   This is a *first draft* based on the 'Thinking about writing processes' section of the unit. Task 5 will probably be the first piece of writing that you would want to collect from the students. We suggest that you **do not grade** this piece of writing, but instead use the ideas found in the writing of all the students to help customise the next lesson plan to your own students' responses. A short comment can be written on each student's answer before it is returned, in order to encourage them to do more thinking-and-writing. This approach is a common one for motivating students to write in exploratory ways. It is also useful at the start of a course for helping you to see the level and needs of the students well before any assessable written work is collected.

### The grammar of academic discourse

**TASKS 6 & 7**   Together these will take 1 to $1^1/_2$ hours.

**Answers for Task 6:**
  1  Non-academic text

| Nominal groups/ pronouns | Precise/ imprecise vocabulary | Active/passive verbs | Point of view |
|---|---|---|---|
| if you agree | its own ways | develops | non-academic: on the basis of the informality of the language used |
| you would say | people from Korea | isn't | |
| its own ways | lots of other things | you would say | |
| | wrong | experts who disagree | |

2 Academic usage examples are circled: you can relate this back to the academic column in Table 1.2, with '1' being a nominal group, '2' being an objective point of view, and '3' concise vocabulary.

> ## Linguistic relativity
> An area of disagreement among experts in the (relationship between language and the mind) (1) is **linguistic relativity**, (also known as) (2) the **Sapir–Whorf hypothesis**, the very popular notion that each language, because of (its linguistic uniqueness) (3), develops its own ways of thinking about the world. For example, if you agree with this opinion you would say that people from Korea 'think differently' from people from Spain because their languages are so different. Even though this belief is popular in many places, there isn't much proof for it. Even experts who disagree about lots of other things often agree that this idea is wrong (Steinberg 1993; Pinker 1994).

**Answers for Task 7:** see suggested text below, i.e. a more formal version.

> The literature review is a critical look at the relevant existing research. It is commonly believed that it is a summary: it is not. Although the writer needs to summarise the relevant research, it is also vital to evaluate this work, show the connections between different work and how it relates to the writer's concerns. In other words, it is not enough for a writer to simply describe an article, it is necessary to select aspects of the work, for example the methodology, and show how it relates to other researchers' methodologies and to the writer's own methodology.

**TASK 8**

1 in order to get the reader's attention. People are attracted by the opportunity to learn something about themselves. This type of opening is commonly associated with magazine articles.

2 A suggested rewrite:
   The way people speak says a lot about them. A dialect or accent might indicate where a person grew up, for instance, while their vocabulary might suggest the type of education they have had. But can the language a person uses – English, Spanish, Mandarin, etc. – indicate the way that person thinks, or help shape their thoughts?

3 These linguistic patterns apparently do not mean that speakers of separate languages perceive colour in different ways.

### The writing process: visualising your text

The material immediately before Task 9 gives you some basic material/ideas to get students started with a process approach to improving their writing. These three concepts: content (material), purpose and audience, are fundamental to decisions about what and how to write. You should discuss this short piece of teaching text with the students, and may wish to develop an activity of your own involving questions about the issues.

**TASK 9**  The first purpose of this task is for issues of academic writing to get thoroughly discussed in the classroom, and for students to have opportunities to ask questions that seem important to them.

The second purpose of the task is for you to get some idea of the students' level of understanding about what academic writing is and why it matters at the very beginning of the course. This will help you to judge how much of the course material in this book you need to use with this group, and whether you need to bring in some supplementary material and exercises. Reading the writing that results will also, of course, help you see the level of language control your students have.

It may be a good idea **not to grade** this piece of writing, but to give some short encouraging comments on it when returning it. (There are some suggestions for this in Appendix C.)

**TASK 10**  You should try to get a clear set of understandings from the head of English programmes in your institution as to what s/he would consider to be a successful attempt at this task – that is, one s/he would respect, take seriously, and may act on. You need not expect the Head of English to read all the students' work. You may find there are examples of good student writing on file that you can refer to; there may be criteria for marking writing in the disciplines of English, psycholinguistics, second language acquisition, psychology or cognitive science that will help you get a 'feel' for how university academics expect students to approach such a task.

This is only the first unit of a course and obviously students are not expected to write well enough to meet the standards expected of regular classes yet. The kinds of feedback that students should be given on this writing should focus on appropriacy of audience, purposes and content and **not** on lower-level aspects of grammar and mechanics. Research has shown that high-level focus, such as suggested here, helps students get the lower-level aspects more correct; and also, that it takes a long time to really improve grammar and mechanics. We want to see students feeling successful and motivated at the end of this unit.

### Follow-up work for students

Students can be encouraged to visit the library at the English Centre (or whatever the unit that teaches English language improvement is called in your institution) and look at the range of books about academic writing, or to visit the main library. It's always a good idea to take a new class around the library to learn how the local system works. You can also encourage them to look on the web for handouts describing the writing expectations of the discipline they are entering, either within your institution or more generally.

# UNIT 2  Teaching notes and Key

## Classification and academic organisation

Classification is an important element in academic writing because it can be applied from intermediate to very advanced levels. Classification is a central concern of many disciplines in the hard and natural sciences, and it is important, too, in social sciences including language studies. The examples in this book are simple ones but the principles will be useful as learners progress.

**Timing:** This part, 'Classification and academic organisation', should take 1–2 hours to complete depending on the level of the students and whether every task is covered. Task 2, for example, could be done by discussion in pairs or group rather than by writing.

## TASK 1

### Being old in the global village

In later life the saying 'no man is an island' becomes truer than ever. Older men and women rely on <u>collective support</u> and this can be divided into three overlapping systems. The first is **economic**, broadly interpreted to include paid and unpaid work. Wherever pensions are low, restricted to civil servants and the military, or non-existent, work is the main means of support in later life. Some elders, usually men, are able to continue in paid jobs, especially if they can shift to easier work, but most are likely to be doing unpaid work such as farming, childcare or housework – often filling in for family members who work in the formal economy.

The second collective support for older people is **the family**. It operates as a workplace, a source of food, shelter and emotional support and, in the last resort, as a care provider. Those who have no family and cannot work must rely wholly on the third system, **formal collectives** – charities and different versions of the welfare state. Welfare in the form of pensions and free healthcare has transformed old age in richer OECD countries and charities ward off destitution for some, but they are not a real safety net.

Each of these three systems is being put at risk by globalisation. The free market capitalism that has accompanied economic globalisation has made rich countries much richer while poor countries have stayed the same or fallen back.

http://www.healthmatters.org.uk/stories/wilson.html#

**TASKS 2 & 3** Any reasonable classification is acceptable. It seems to us that 'education' stands alone in this list, but some students might be able to convincingly argue for a classification that puts education and movies together, for example. Task 2 is directly related to Task 1: the emphasis is on thinking through writing and not writing for accuracy. This writing should not be collected and marked/graded.

**TASK 4** 'this can be divided into' (para 1)
'the first'…, 'the second'… 'the third system'…

**TASK 5**

| There are | two | types<br>classes<br>**kinds**<br>categories<br>sorts<br>varieties | of effects | resulting from globalisation |
|---|---|---|---|---|

| The effects | are<br>may be<br>can be | classified | **according to**<br>on the basis of …<br>depending upon … |
|---|---|---|---|

| The effects of globalisation | may be<br>can be | grouped<br>**divided** | into three main categories |
|---|---|---|---|

**TASK 6** Accept any reasonable answers. Here are some suggestions.
1 Business
Operating in more than one country: global corporation, multinational
Operating in one country: local company, regional enterprise
2 Religions
Monotheistic: Islam, Judaism and Christianity
Other: Buddhism
Sects in Islam: Sunni and Shia
Sects in Christianity: Catholicism and Protestantism
3 Audio equipment: CD player, speakers and amplifier
Software: CDs

**TASK 7**
1 The religions of the world can be divided into those who believe in the existence of one god, Judaism, Christianity and Islam, and those who do not, for example, Buddhism. Religions are often divided into sects. In Islam the main divisions are between Sunni and Shia sects, while Christianity is divided into Catholicism and Protestantism.
2 One way of categorising business is according to its physical location. Global and multinational businesses operate in more than one country, while regional and local business operate within a country.

3 Audio equipment involves hardware (CD player, speakers and amplifiers) and software, CDs.

### Using data classifications to create visuals and/or texts

Often, visual presentation works very well for classifications, especially when they are complex.

If the students do all 8–12 it will take more than two hours. Tasks 11 and 12 are advanced; with an intermediate group the teacher can instead have students write a text for the same audience about politeness in English. The task can also be simplified by asking them to write about only **one** politeness formula.

**TASK 8** You should read the sample answer to Task 9 to prepare for the discussion in Task 8. In our own opinion, the diagram is more effective than the written text.

**TASK 9** Possible text: 7 sentences (could be 5/6 or more than 7)

Language can be divided into two main types: audio/oral (spoken) and visual language. There are two kinds of visual language: graphic and non-graphic, which consists of facial expression, body gesture, etc.

Graphic language is more complex, consisting of verbal, pictorial and schematic language. Verbal language means writing; pictorial language refers to things like drawings and photographs. Schematic language includes charts, diagrams and musical notations.

We can classify written language into handwritten and machine-written language. 'Machine written' refers to print, typescript (these days usually by computer) and another text form.

**TASK 10** Accept any graphic display that makes sense. 'Apologies' and 'response to apologies' could be linked together as could 'greetings' and 'farewells'.

**TASK 11** **Students are given the choice of completing either Part A or B.**

    **A** Encourage students to use their personal experiences with English.

    *Response to greetings*: echo the formula; or use a 'universal' politeness query [How are you? Good to see you.]; or use an idiom [e.g. What's up?]

    *Reply to introductions*: Echo the formula; use an idion [e.g. Fine, thanks. And you?]

    *Response to thanks*: You're welcome (AmE); Don't mention it (BrE); or use an idiom [e.g. No sweat (AmE), No worries (AusE)]

    **B** This task is more advanced; however, it is good preparation for Task 12. This task is fairly straightforward with a monolingual class, where groups can work together, and where you are also a speaker of that language, or at least a second language user of it. With multilingual classes, you may adapt this task and make it a little easier by providing students with an organisational structure for their visual:

Greetings
[Response to greetings]
Farewells
Introductions
Toasts
Congratulations
Thanks
[Response to thanks]
Seasonal greetings
Apologies
[Response to apologies ]

**TASK 12** If your students do this task, you will want to spend half an hour in a later lesson, after you have read all their texts, discussing the strengths and weaknesses of what they have written from the point of view of content/meaning as well as language accuracy.

There is no sample text for Task 12 in this Key. Obviously it will vary for every language. You need to prepare for this task by writing your own sample text, and ideally by getting some comments from colleagues and people with a good knowledge of the language in question.

## Organising the research paper

**TASK 13** Conventionally the four key components of a research paper are Introduction, Method, Results, and Discussion (IMRD: see Swales, Genre Analysis, 1990). Most research papers have other components as well, but these four are virtually always the core organisational elements. The literature review is usually present but does not directly add to the original research. The Conclusion is a rhetorical 'extra' and again does not directly add to the research's originality.

| | |
|---|---|
| 1.The New Wave of Globalization and Its Economic Effects 23 | Previous waves of globalization and reversals<br>The new wave of globalization |
| 2. Improving the International Architecture for Integration 53 | Open economies have more competition and firm turnover<br>The investment climate affects the benefits of openness<br>Integration with the world economy affects employment and wages<br>Social protection in globalizing economies<br>Summary of recommendations |
| 3. Strengthening Domestic Institutions and Policies 85 | Trade policy<br>Policies for capital flows to developing countries<br>Policies toward migration<br>Summary of recommendations |
| 4. Power, Culture, and the Environment 121 | Globalization and power<br>Globalization and culture<br>Globalization and the environment<br>Summary of recommendations |
| 5. An Agenda for Action 145 | Anxieties and their foundation<br>Building an inclusive world economy: An agenda for action |

### Recording your Internet explorations

If you do this part wholly in class meeting time, it will take 3–5 hours of class time. However, you may prefer to take your group to the library or to a computer lab on campus to begin this task, as many teachers do, to ensure that everyone can use the technology and understands the task, before setting them to do the exploration out of class time.

**TASK 15**   Prepare for this task by making sure you know your institution's URL and by exploring its possibilities yourself. If you are in a tertiary institution, you'll probably find an English language centre or student support services unit that will have useful information, or at least some links to useful information. If you are in a school, you may need to explore links to local and regional tertiary institutions, teachers' organisations and governmental support units for English language teachers.

There are no correct answers; however your goal is for students to end up with some links to resources that they can use later for help with their writing. You can build up your own set of resources by recording all the best links/pages that your students locate, for future classes you teach. If students do the second suggested task, it makes sense that they would choose something relating either to problems of globalisation or to problems and solutions for students learning to write English as a second language.

**TASK 16**   We suggest that you find some relevant activity or task that will encourage students to write in their e-journal at least once a week. Considerable research has shown that frequent writing, even without correction or feedback, does lead to writing improvement. It also makes sense that the writing students do in their e-journals relates to work they will be doing later on in their English courses.

**TASK 17**   We suggest that you treat this as a formal writing task and that it should be graded. Remind the students of what they learned in Unit 1 under 'Distinguishing between academic and personal styles of writing'. Refer to Appendix B.

# UNIT 3 Teaching notes and Key

### Exploring comparison and contrast structures

**Timing:** Tasks 1–4 will take $1^1/_2$–2 hours

This first part of the unit introduces two main ways of developing a description based on comparison and contrast. This section can be dealt with by getting students to compare two items they are familiar with, e.g. two cities in your country. On the board, build up two descriptions: one based on the AAA–BBB pattern, the other based on the AB–AB–AB pattern. Ask students:
- What is different about the two descriptions?
- What are the advantages and disadvantages of the two patterns?

**Differences:** the AAA–BBB pattern does not use comparative forms such as *bigger than*, *more comfortable than*, etc. As a result, readers have to switch back and forth between the paragraphs to figure out the comparisons and contrasts.

| Pattern | Advantages | Disadvantages |
|---------|-----------|---------------|
| AAA–BBB | easier to write | comparisons/contrasts are not explicit |
| AB–AB–AB | comparisons/contrasts are made explicit | requires use of comparatives |

**TASK 1** Text 1: clearly an example of AAA–BBB.
Text 2: the use of *On the other hand* shows it is intended as an example of AB–AB–AB.
Text 3: clearly an example of AB–AB–AB.

**TASK 2** The answers to this task depend on the kinds of fruit and vegetables that are considered stereotypical in your culture.

| Feature | Fruits | Vegetables |
|---------|--------|------------|
| Contain seeds | +/– | + |
| Pleasant smell | + | +/– |
| Sweet taste | + | +/– |

**TASK 3** Answers will depend on the local culture. Here is an example.

| Spices and herbs | From your country or region | From another country or region |
|---|---|---|
| chilli | chilli cooked with beef and kidney beans | chilli added to other spices and used in the cooking of fish, meat, vegetables, etc. |

Students may need to discuss this with each other; or, in a mixed-background class, they may need to plan ahead and ask family members or look on the Web. Although this is a motivating task, it should be kept to a reasonably short length of class time.

**TASK 4**

| (1) wealthier | (4) comparing | (7) cost | (10) costing |
|---|---|---|---|
| (2) somewhat more expensive | (5) generally of lower quality | (8) much higher | (11) difference |
| (3) higher | (6) are different from | (9) lower | (12) would cost |

## The language of comparison and contrast

**Timing:** This is a major teaching section and will take 3–4 hours excluding the writing time given to students, in or out of class. Tasks 9 and 12 are writing tasks: only one of them should be evaluated. Task 15 is an optional writing task which you may choose to give to stronger writers.

**TASK 5** **Contrasts:** there are a large number of these possible, e.g.: *The average growth rate of GNP per capita for the period 1994–1998 was higher for Finland than for the United States.*
**Comparisons:** these need to be approximate (rather than specific), e.g.: *The bread and cereal price index in 1998 was similar in Austria and Belgium.*

**TASK 6**

| Comparison between sentences | Contrast between sentences |
|---|---|
| 1, 4, 6 | 2, 3, 5 |

**TASK 7** To complete this task, AAA–BBB students need to write preferably **two** paragraphs; while AB–AB–AB students should aim for **one** paragraph.

**TASK 8** Get students to state their personal preferences.
Ask if it is important to be *explicit* regarding comparisons and contrasts in an encyclopaedia entry.
Ask which text is more interesting to read.

**TASK 9**  1 **Write a text:** Depending on your location, not all of the recommendations will be relevant. For example, students living near the equator will always have sufficient exposure to sunlight. In view of this, it would be a good idea to ask students to read the advice and discuss which points would make a difference for them.

Refer to Appendix C for ideas on responding to students' writing. Remember to balance a concern with language accuracy with the need for students to show they have seriously engaged with the ideas in the text and with their own reactions and ideas.

2 **Develop and administer a questionnaire:** This task is more suitable for graduate students as creating a questionnaire will take at least 1–2 hours and then the work of collecting responses begins. This activity brings home to students the real contrasts between people's views.

*Using comparisons and contrasts to evaluate and recommend*

**TASK 10**  Possible answers include: quality, attractiveness, taste, health promoting, hygiene, environmentally friendly, ease of preparation, etc.

**TASK 11**  Text A: frequency of personal preference, health criteria (fat content)
Text B: costs (not stated); benefits: range of choice, quality, hygiene
Text C: time in relation to percentage of income spent on food

**TASK 12**  Students will need to decide which organisational pattern they will use. They should be asked to produce an introduction, the body of the text, and a conclusion giving their evaluation of trends in convenience foods.
  Depending on the amount of time available or the frequency of class meetings, you might expect students to spend more time on either the first part of Task 9 (writing a text) or Task 12.

**TASK 13**  (1) evaluations (2) evaluates (3) recommendations

Make sure that students have grasped the idea of progressing from *compare* to *evaluate* to *recommend*.

**TASK 14**  We <u>recommend</u> …
… the regulatory authorities <u>will also need to</u> analyse …
We therefore <u>recommend</u> …
… <u>should be commissioned</u> by the …
… <u>should consider</u> those of the following points

## The research paper

**Timing:** 1 hour

| TASK 15 | claiming that the research to be undertaken is central to the area | making generalisations about a topic | reviewing items of previous research |
|---|---|---|---|
| | 1, 9 | 2, 3, 4, 6, 7, 8, 10 | 5 |

| TASK 16 | claiming that there is a gap in the previous research | making a counter-claim (i.e. claiming that previous work in this research area was wrong) | raising a question about a theory, previous research, etc. | continuing a tradition |
|---|---|---|---|---|
| | 2, 3, 4, 7, 8 | 10 | 5, 6, | 1, 9, 11 |

**TASK 17**

1  a, b and c.
2  The first four sentences establish the central role that food intake and preferences play in the wellbeing of hospitalised geriatric patients. The rest of the first paragraph narrows the generalisations down to focus on Malaysia, and begins some general review of previous research.

Notice that the second paragraph follows a similar structure.

**TASK 18**

1  'It appeared that there was a need to investigate the adequacy of dietary intake and food preferences among our hospitalised geriatric patients.' (paragraph 3)
2  b)

**TASK 19**  Yes.

## The writing process: Joining a virtual peer group to get feedback on your writing

**Timing:** 1 hour, if prepared in class. Complete for homework.

**TASK 20**  Encourage students to use comparisons and contrasts where possible in this essay. Also encourage them to evaluate the advice they find and to make recommendations. Remember, and remind students, that this is part of a sequence of tasks relating to getting feedback on writing.

# UNIT 4 Teaching notes and Key

**TASK 1**  The definition that is factually incorrect is:

AIDS is a disease that affects a very <u>small</u> number of people each year.

**TASK 2**  The web will provide a range of satisfactory definitions for all these terms. Ask the students to give the source of the definition they propose.

a) **Fitness** is the ability to carry out daily tasks with vigour and alertness without undue fatigue and with ample energy to enjoy leisure-time pursuits and to meet unforeseen emergencies.

b) **Cholesterol** is a soft, waxy substance found among the lipids (fats) in the bloodstream and in all the body's cells.

c) **Nutrition** is the process by which an individual takes in and utilises food material.

d) **Disease** is disorder of bodily function or destructive processes in organs, organs' systems or in an organism with recognisable signs and symptoms.

e) **Sanitation** is a process capable of reducing the number of microbial contaminants to a relatively safe level.

f) **Antibiotics** are medications which can destroy or inhibit the growth of bacteria.

**TASK 3**  **Health** is 'a state of complete physical, mental and social well-being and not merely the absence of disease or infirmity'.

This is the World Health Organization definition, in force since 1948, and probably not found very satisfactory by many medical professionals. Discussion among students may generate some richer definitions, and it is good to encourage this. Short definitions have to be simple and so they are not always completely satisfactory.

**TASK 4**  **Memory** is the ability to retain information. [In their definitions, students may also refer to the time periods over which information can be recalled.] A fuller definition, less dependent on the text, might be 'the cognitive processes whereby past experience is remembered'.

**TASK 5**  A **placebo** is an inactive substance which may look like medicine but contains no medicine.

**TASK 6** 1  a)  Students of different abilities and subject knowledge will suggest a range of definitions from:
A *Chronic disease* is an illness that lasts for a long time
to
A *Chronic disease* is a disease which has one or more of the following characteristics: is permanent, leaves residual disability; is caused by non-reversible pathological alternation, requires special training of the patient for rehabilitation, or may be expected to require a long period of supervision, observation, or care.

   b)  This part of the task will reinforce the message that: Specialised definitions are useful for students in those disciplinary areas, while short and simple definitions are useful for lay people.

**TASK 7** Check that the sentences containing restrictive and non-restrictive sentences, respectively, begin in the following order:
a)  Hypochondria is …
    Hypochondria, …
b)  Energy is …
    Energy, …
c)  The World Health Organization, …
    The World Health Organization is …
d)  Acupuncture is …
    Acupuncture,
e)  Vision, …
    Vision is …

**TASK 8** The following are acceptable suggestions; students, especially those with specialist knowledge, may have equally good alternatives.
1  A **scar** is a mark left on the skin by injury.
2  **Hair** is a dense growth of fibrous substances that helps to prevent heat loss.
3  **Smell** is the sensation that results when the nose is stimulated by chemicals in the atmosphere.
4  **Genes** are segments of DNA considered to be key units of heredity.
5  A **calorie** is a measure of energy commonly used in the physical sciences.

**TASK 9** As with all such tasks, there is a range of good possibilities. Encourage students to find **several** points of similarity and/or difference. Here is one suggestion.

The WHO, Ayurveda and Chinese definitions are all positive, whereas the biomedical definition focuses on treatment of disease, which is a negative way of thinking about "health." However, the WHO shows its biomedical influences when it stresses that health is "not merely the absence of disease". The Ayurveda and the Chinese approaches both use a wider understanding of health than the WHO does, and understand that being healthy may be defined differently for each individual. Ayurveda and Chinese medicine both recognize subtle states of imbalance within the individual as showing lack of, or loss of, health even before western medicine would define the individual as unhealthy or showing signs of disease.

**TASK 10**  Accept any variation on the following.

| *Chronic diseases* | *Acute diseases* |
|---|---|
| usually emerge slowly | emerge rapidly |
| last a long time | short duration |
| may be mild or severe | may be very severe |
| may come and go, or remain constant | remain constant |
| may have no obvious cause | have an obvious cause |
| do not affect heart or breathing rate | increase heart and breathing rates |
| do not raise blood pressure | raise blood pressure |
| interfere with sleep | |
| decrease appetite | |
| may cause depression | |

**TASK 11**  a) Good dental health in children can be identified by the appearance of the teeth, which are well-aligned, not crowded, and white in colour; by the absence of dental decay or gum disease; and by proper function of the teeth and jaw.

b) Periodontal (gum) disease is not included in most definitions of good dental health because it is not commonly found in children.

**TASK 12**  Teachers will find that a careful search of the World Wide Web will enable them to judge the content of all students' answers. We advise that teachers direct their students to write for 'the educated lay person' and not for other specialists, in order to make sure that the answers are not too technical for people outside the field (including the teacher) to understand or judge. If you mark this writing, be sure to give a specific percentage of the marks for the content/facts and another specific percentage for the correct use of language.

**TASK 13**  A useful website on stress is http://www.ivf.com/stress.html

Sample definition: Stress is a state of mental or emotional strain or suspense.

A longer definition might be: Stress is the non-specific response of the body to any demand made upon it which results in physiological symptoms such as a rise in the blood pressure, release of hormones, quickness of breath, tightening of muscles, perspiration, and increased cardiac activity. Stress may be negative or positive. Stress may keep a person motivated and alert, while too little stress can lead to inattention and underperformance. However, too much stress, particularly over a prolonged period of time, can trigger mental and physical health problems, which are negative.

**TASK 14** The webpage cited in the task has 4 areas of test anxiety information:

- *Common symptoms of test anxiety*
- *What can be done?*
- *Tips for test taking*
- *Strategies for doing your best in an exam*

These can be used as the organising areas for the clustering task. Students will find other information and will probably come up with some of their own – this should be encouraged. Here is a possible cluster-map resulting from this task, but there are many possible variations and no right answers.

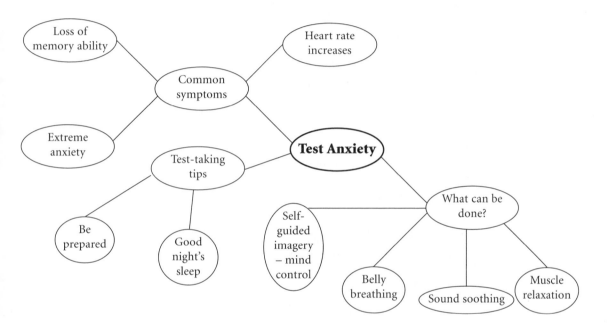

Look at the grouping the students have done. Consider whether they have used what they learned in Units 2 and 3 about classes and categories, and about making comparisons and contrasts, to help them arrange sensible groups to identify/classify defining features. Suggest any necessary changes to make their pre-writing more useful for writing a text. This pre-writing process works most effectively when several classmates or students from other similar courses work together, and when you are available to give the students suggestions and guidance but not 'answers'.

**TASK 15** This writing task can be collected for formal assessment, either immediately or after a draft-review process. The expectations are demanding in terms of both content and organisation, but there is room for some creativity by the students. Refer to Appendix B for ideas about judging writing.

# UNIT 5 Teaching notes and Key

**The Honesty Principle**

The aim of this section is to learn how generalisations are used to organise a piece of writing. It also covers the relationship between a generalisation, the 'Honesty Principle' and the need to 'hedge' or 'boost' claims made in the generalisation.

**TASK 1**

**Text A**

Generalisation: The latest Government Social Trends reports show ... their early 20s.
Comparison: There were 87 births ... in the same year.

**Text B**

Generalisation: World population growth ... 1900–1994 period.
Classification: These are as follows ... 2.4 per cent + (Middle East, Western Asia, Africa).

**Text C**

Generalisation: Vietnam has a ... care system. Example: Its incidence of infant mortality is relatively low.

**Text D**

Contrast: (On the other hand) Wholegrains such as wholemeal bread, brown rice and wholewheat pasta limit the amount of insulin the body produces.

**TASK 2**

The text that most needs further support is Text A (*UK Demographic Trends*). Further information can be found at, for example, http://www.statistics.gov.uk/cci/nugget.asp?id=951
The information at this site and related links will also help students think about later tasks in this unit, especially Task 12.

**TASK 4**

a) A result of the gross disagreement between researchers. (This text should be written out separately by student.)
b) Consanguinity is defined as ... and detectable ancestor. (This text should be circled by student.)
c) There is no common consensus ... of their offspring. (This text should be underlined by student.)
d) However, in this regard it is possible ... schools of thought. (This text should have 'class' written alongside by student.)

**TASK 6**   1  a)  The German population could have shrunk due to … ; Increased emigration may also be a …

  b)  As he is describing the present, 'Germany is experiencing …', perhaps there is no evidence as yet available to support a more certain claim. This is an example of the Honesty Principle at work.

  2  a)  However, in this regard it is possible to recognize …

  b)  As an academic, the writer needs to group many items into fewer categories to help make sense of them.

**TASK 7**   Table 5.1 Examples of language for hedging generalisations

| Degree of certainty | | Quantity | Frequency | Adjectives | Adverbs | Verbs |
|---|---|---|---|---|---|---|
| **Complete** | | all/every/each no/none/ not any | **(1) always** <br><br> never | definite certain undoubted clear | **(2) certainly** definitely undoubtedly clearly | will/will not **(3) is**/are (not) <br><br> must have to |
| **Partial** | *high* | a majority (of) **(4) many**/ much | usual(ly) normal(ly) general(ly) as a rule on the whole often | probable likely | presumably probably/ probable likely | should would ought to |
| | | some/ several a number of | frequent(ly) <br> sometimes occasional(ly) | uncertain | **(5) possible** possibly perhaps maybe | can/cannot **(6) could/ could not** may/may not might/might not |
| | *low* | a minority a few /a little few/little | rare(ly) seldom hardly ever **(7) scarcely ever** | unlikely **(8) improbable** | | |
| Impersonal (i.e. no commitment from writer) | | There is evidence to suggest that … <br> It is said that … <br> X reports that … | | | | |

**TASK 8**
1 Scientists believe/suggest/speculate/estimate/think/argue/indicate/project/forecast.
2 The figures suggest/indicate that …
3 When a region is hit by a food shortage, the inhabitants seem to/appear to/tend to migrate.
4 Two-thirds of the world's population seem to/appear to/are thought to/are believed to/are estimated to live …
5 There seems to be/appears to be three …

**TASK 9**
1 a) This is a neutral statement of fact: there is disagreement. We do not know how large or small the division is.
   b) This statement tells us that the division is very large.
2 The sentences that have been boosted are a) and c).
The reasons for boosting sentence 'a' is that the researcher may have wished to stress the methodology as, on this occasion, the expected results were not achieved.
The reasons for boosting sentence 'c' is to stress the point in the hope that it will generate/encourage action (by teachers?) in response.

**TASK 10**
(1) completely/strongly
(2) completely/strongly
(3) completely/highly
(4) deep
(5) thorough

**TASK 11**
1 almost
2 is forecast
3 close
4 well
5 vastly
6 is projected

**TASK 12**   **Boosters**
<u>detailed</u> picture of the history …
will have been measured to <u>high</u> precision,
and we will know <u>lots</u> of other facts …
in fact it will be <u>old fashioned</u> to consider ….

**Neutral**
By the middle of the … certainly have a clear/good picture of …
The parameters in our … measured to precision, and we will know a considerable/respectable/reasonable number of other …
In fact it will be out of favour/unusual to consider …

**Hedged**

By the middle of the … we will presumably/possibly/probably/likely have a clear/good picture of …

The parameters in our … should/ought/might/may have been measured to precision, and we should/ought to/may/might know a considerable/respectable/reasonable number of other …

In fact it could/may/might be unusual/out of favour to consider …

TASK 13

1  a)  The graph shows that the world population is increasing.
   b)  The rate at which the world population is increasing is slowing down.
   c)  Data from 1950–2000 approx. (half the data).
   d)  Data from approx. 2000–2050 (half the data).

2  Here is a sample answer, with suitable key words shown in **bold**.

The first graph **shows that** between 1950 and approx 2000 the world population increased steadily, and it **suggests that** the increase **will** continue in the next fifty years. However, the second graph **shows that** the rate at which the world population is increasing is slowing down (or, has been slowing down since the 1960s). It **predicts that** by 2040 the rate of population growth **will only be** approx. 0.5% a year. **If** the trend in the second graph continues, **it is likely that** by 2100 the population of the world **will be** at or below replacement level.

## Writing a literature review

TASK 14

2  a)  describe the evidence for the reader
4  b)  suggest why they found no interaction

Remind students that there is no general rule about what is included in a literature review, **except** that it must be directly **relevant** to the topic or research question of the main research being reported.

TASK 15

Overcrowding results in problems which are annoying but not necessarily fatal. Overpopulation, on the other hand, can result in fatalities because resources (food, etc.) are less than required.

## The writing process: Working with a peer group

The aim of this section is to engage students in a collaborative writing process. This will help to make them more aware of what is involved in the writing process.

**TASKS 16 & 17** For these tasks it would be a good idea to limit the peer group (four students) to four printed and four Internet resources. Here are some useful points to remember.

### Managing the process
- Have students draw up a timetable for the various stages of the investigation.
- Set a deadline for the completion of the work.
- Arrange to meet each group at appropriate times to review progress and discuss difficulties. This could be in class while groups continue their work on the task, or in fixed out-of-class consultation hours.
- Emphasize to the peer groups that, as the learning progresses and the clusters start to be more fully developed and understood, it may be necessary to adjust the responsibilities: some sub-topics may turn out not to be worth pursuing; others may need to be divided into two areas. Each group member ought to have about the same amount of work to do.

### Ensuring effective texts get written
- Emphasise that information should be summarised in the student's own words rather than directly quoted.
- Guide students to focus on organisation of the complete text at the later stages; the result should not look like 4–5 separate summaries cut-and-pasted end to end!

**Marking:** principles for assessing students' writing are in Appendix C. However, when marking the work done by groups it is important to be confident that all students have made a fair contribution; this is easiest when you have met each group several times, however briefly. Some teachers ask each student to write a peer group evaluation describing how the group worked and what, if any, problems arose.

# UNIT 6 Teaching notes and Key

**TASK 1**

> First millennium (1000 BC) Celts

> Romans arrive 43 BC

> 410 Romans leave

> Anglo-Saxon invasions

**TASK 2**  1st C: Angles, Saxons and Jutes invaded England
5th–8th C: Four main spoken dialects of English developed
7th and 8th C: Northumbria's culture and language dominated Britain
9th C: Vikings made Northumbria, Kentish, and Mercia dependent
10th Century: West Saxon dialect the official language of Britain
10th C: Written Old English developed

**TASK 3**  The forward slashes below indicate alternative or additional answers.
  (1)  Then/ at that time/up to that time
  (2)  In
  (3)  then
  (4)  until
  (5)  In
  (6)  since
  (7)  By
  (8)  now
  (9)  to
  (10)  Since
  (11)  during
  (12)  At that time/During that time
  (13)  still

**TASK 4**  The students' answers are listed below on the left – they were simply asked
for 'past', 'present' or 'future' as answers. Alongside each answer, in square
brackets, is the more detailed name for the tense in case the students
require a more detailed explanation.
  (1)  present [present continuous]
  (2)  future [future with 'will']
  (3)  past [past simple passive]
  (4)  present [present simple]
  (5)  present [present simple]

(6)  present [present simple]
(7)  past [past simple]
(8)  past [past simple]
(9)  present [present simple]
(10) past [past simple passive]
(11) past [past simple passive]
(12) past [past simple]
(13) past [past simple]
(14) past [past simple]
(15) past [past perfect]
(16) past [past perfect]
(17) past [past simple]
(18) past [past simple]
(19) past [past simple]
(20) past [past simple]
(21) past [past simple]
(22) past [past simple]
(23) present [present simple passive]

**TASK 5**  Probably to get the reader's attention by showing how this topic *Gondwanaland* has relevance for the present. Our planet is still changing and will continue to do so. *(Therefore we should study how the planet has changed in the past.)*

'Gondwanaland' (named after an aboriginal tribe in India, the Gonds) is a proposed ancient super-continent that (3) was comprised of the land masses that ...

**TASK 6**  The underlined italicised verbs are the correct answers (ignore the non-italicised underlined words).

> Recent estimates <u>place</u> current global forest cover at about 50% of its original extent, and <u>conclude</u> that a large proportion of this loss <u>has occurred</u> within the past 50 years. Despite conservation efforts, many remaining forest ecosystems *have been* seriously degraded and fragmented, resulting in environmentally, economically and aesthetically impoverished landscapes. Loss of forest cover not only *limits* the scope of biodiversity conservation but also *diminishes* the prospect for attaining secure livelihoods among many rural populations throughout the developing world.
>
> Forest restoration *has been identified* in several contexts as a key activity for reversing the trend of forest loss and improving biodiversity conservation, ecosystem functions and improved livelihood security.
>
> [Extracted from http://www.unep-wcmc.org/forest/restoration/index.htm retrieved 27/2/04]

**TASK 7**

1  c
2  b
3  f
4  a
5  d
6  g
7  e

**TASK 8**

1  (1)  This
   (2)  they
   (3)  It
   (4)  This
   (5)  it
   (6)  it
   (7)  these
   (8)  they
   (9)  one
   (10) its
   (11) Ours
   (12) we

2  The examples of repetition are circled in the text below.

Tropical forest is being destroyed at the rate of 40,000 square miles = an area the size of Ohio, per year. ......(1)...... is mainly due to slash-and-burn agriculture in areas of high population growth, in which small areas are cleared and used for a few years until ......(2)...... become infertile, and then more acreage is cleared. About 44% of the original tropical forest on the earth is now gone. ......(3)...... has been estimated that 15–20% of all species will become extinct by the year 2000 because of the destruction of tropical forests ......(4)...... rate is about 10,000 times as high as the rate prior to the existence of human beings.

The fundamental reason for the degradation and loss of habitat is the explosive growth of the human population. Since 1900 ......(5)...... has more than tripled. Since 1950 ......(6)...... has more than doubled, to 6 billion. Every year 90 million more people (= 3x the population of California) are added to the planet. All of ......(7)...... people need places to live, work and play, and ......(8)...... all contribute to habitat loss and global pollution.

Our generation is the first ......(9)...... to really become aware of the fact that the human population is causing irreparable damage to the planet – to the air, water and soil of the planet and to ......(10)...... biological resources. ......(11)...... is not the first generation to do damage to the planet, but ......(12)...... are the first to realize the extent of the problem.

[From: Biodiversity and Conservation: A Hypertext Book by Peter J. Bryant http://darwin.bio.uci.edu/~sustain/bio65/lec01/b65lec01.htm]

**TASK 9** As always with writing tasks, there are many possible appropriate answers: here is one possibility.

Americans use more than one billion pounds of pesticides annually to combat pests in agriculture, homes and all public places. The health effects of this pesticide exposure range from mild to severe and may include dizziness and nausea to more severe effects such as acute poisoning and cancer. In many cases the effects are not immediate, but may show up later as unexplained illnesses.

The number of cases of pesticide exposure in the U.S. is alarming. In 1997, 88,255 emergency cases were reported to the national network of Poison Control Centers, and of these, fourteen fatalities were attributed to pesticide poisoning. Over 50 per cent of all reported cases of pesticide poisoning cases involve children under six years of age. A 1998 study showed that effected children often have impaired memory and hand-eye coordination, as well as decreased stamina. When compared to an unexposed peer, they had difficulty in drawing a simple picture of a person.

**TASK 10** You will probably find this works best if you go through the diagram with the students. The correct sequence is given below. [Retrieved from www.handprint.com/LS/ANC/evol.html chart]

Note that students need only report the <u>main</u> hominid developments.

| History of Man | |
|---|---|
| SPECIES | TIME PERIOD |
| Ardipithocus ramidus | 5 to 4.2 million years ago |
| Australopithecus anamensis | 4.2 to 3.9 million years ago |
| Australopithecus afarensis | 4 to 2.9 million years ago |
| Australopithecus africanus | 3 to 2.2 million years ago |
| Australopithecus robustus | 2.0 to 1.6 million years ago |
| Homo habilis | 2.2 to 1.6 million years ago |
| Homo ergaster | 1.8 to 1.2 million years ago |
| Homo erectus | 2.0 to 0.4 million years ago |
| Homo heidelbergensis | 900 to 200 thousand years ago |
| Homo sapiens neanderthalensis | 150 to 30 thousand years ago |
| Homo sapiens sapiens | 50 thousand years ago to present |

**TASK 11**  As always with writing tasks, there are many possible appropriate answers: here is one possibility.

Fossils have been found that are about 4.5 million years old, and they suggest that **hominids**, who would eventually become the ancestors of humans, started to become differentiated about five million years ago. But the first fossils that could really be called human-like date from only about 350,000 years ago. The Neanderthals (*H. sapiens neanderthalensis*) were the hominids most closely resembling modern humans, and the fossils that have been found suggest that they lived between 150,000–30,000 years ago. What we would recognise as actual humans (*H. sapiens sapiens*) evolved about 50,000–35,000 years ago. *H. sapiens neanderthalensis* and *H. sapiens sapiens* lived at the same time for about 20,000 years.

**TASK 12**
1 critically imperiled, imperiled and vulnerable
2 secure/apparently secure
3 (a) illustrates/shows
  (b) 68%
  (c) 15%
  (d) danger/threat
  (e) 1
4    (o)

**TASK 13**
1 Those that live in water.
2 Freshwater mussels/freshwater fish
3 Amphibians (36%)/birds (14%)
4 Complete this summary of the data:

The answers are given in **bold** type in the text below.

> The data show the state of selected **species** relative to the four in-danger categories, vulnerable, imperiled, critically imperiled and presumed extinct. We can divide the species into **three** types: those that live on **land**, those that exist in water and those that exist on land and in **water**. In terms of the four in-danger categories, the water species are the focus of most concern with 69% of **freshwater mussels** in most danger followed by crayfish (51%), stoneflies (43%), freshwater fish (37%) and **amphibians** (36%). Land species, on the other hand, are **less** imperiled with only 14% and 16% of birds and mammals in any danger, and reptiles, butterflies/Skippers, Tiger Beetles, ferns, gymnosperms and flowering plants at between 18% and **33%**.

**TASK 14**  Preparatory task only. The linked text can be seen on the website. Another useful website is www.nationalgeographic.com

**TASK 15** Note that some word choice problems, stylistic awkwardness, and tense errors have been deliberately introduced into this mock student text. Most of the mock 'peer review' here is a matter of opinion or preference more than correctness. You, as teacher, will be able to identify all the absolute errors. Remember that student reviewers probably will not get everything right, but they are not marking, only commenting and giving views and suggestions. The comments, deletions and replacement text are all shown in **bold** type.

Over half of the world's forests have been destroyed, and the current alarming rate of deforestation ~~is~~ **seems to be getting** ~~worst~~ **worse**. Every minute an amount of land **THIS IS VAGUE – BETTER WORD CHOICE WOULD IMPROVE IT** about equal to 37 football pitches ~~gets~~ **becomes** deforested and soon we will be left with a planet ~~empty of~~ **without** trees. But the world's forests are the home of many of the most important species on earth. **SHOULD YOU START A SENTENCE WITH "BUT"?**

Forests also play a vital role in regulating the climate and making the planet habitable. **WHY IS THIS SENTENCE ALL BY ITSELF?**

Once upon a time much of the earth was covered in trees, but the growing human population has killed **INCORRECT TENSE** most of them **them=what?**. This **what?** happened a long time ago in countries with mild climates like Britain and other parts of Europe because humans started growing crops several thousand years ago, and agriculture has now reduced the great European forests to tiny pockets here and there. **THIS SENTENCE IS NOT VERY CLEAR**

But the tropical forests only became threatened since **TENSE ERROR** the last century. There was twice as much tropical forest at the turn of the 20th century as there is today, and it **UNCLEAR** is disappearing fast. In Africa about four million hectares of forest got **"GOT" IS NOT A GOOD ACADEMIC STYLE WORD AND IS ALSO A TENSE ERROR** destroyed each year, and now 45 per cent of its original forest cover has disappeared. **GOOD TENSE USE**

Deforestation is caused by commercial logging, clearance for roads and railways, forest fires, mining and drilling. Ordinary people also cut down trees for agriculture, fuelwood collection and to make space for homes, and it's hard to know who is to blame for it. **UNCLEAR PRO-FORMS; AND, DOES THIS PARAGRAPH HAVE A POINT? CAN YOU MAKE IT CLEARER?**

People have been living in and around tropical rainforests for tens of thousands of years. **NICE SENTENCE** However, in the last two centuries populations have expanded, and did need **INCORRECT PAST FORM** more and more space for housing and agriculture and more wood for building. As richer countries have demanded more hard woods from tropical rainforests the problem has become even greater. **WHICH PROBLEM?**

**THIS ESSAY SEEMS TO FINISH WITHOUT AN ACTUAL CONCLUSION**

**TASKS 16 & 17** These are process tasks and there are no answers. Each student's text will be different. The learning objective is for students to understand and be comfortable with the **process** of giving and getting feedback from classmates. The teaching objective is to make the process go smoothly so that students can understand how peer review works effectively.

**A note on marking**
You are encouraged to take the peer review into account in responding to the essays. If you do formal marking on this writing, you are encouraged to take the peer feedback into account in your marking scheme.

# UNIT 7 Teaching notes and Key

**TASK 1**
1 <u>The process of erosion occurs when the surface of the land is worn and lost</u>.
2 There are many specific types of erosion. [circled]
3 Four
4 The Present Tense
5 a) Not used
   b) Used 10 times: occurs, are, remove, occurs, happens, is, bounces, moves, occurs, blows.
   c) Used 4 times: is worn away, (is) lost, are formed, is removed.
   d) Not used
6 b) The Present Simple Tense
   c) The Present Simple Passive Tense

**TASK 2**
1 First/Firstly/First of all/To begin with
2 Secondly
3 Thirdly
4 Next/After that/Then
5 Finally/Lastly
6 After that/Next/Then
7 Finally/Lastly

**TASK 3**
1 The majority of verbs are in the Present Simple Active Tense; the remainder are in the Present Simple Passive.
2 begin, starting, the first stage, the second stage, finally, firstly, next, the final event, as (this warm air rises), then, in the meantime.

**TASK 4**
Here is the sequence of the original text.
1 C [given as the example]
2 B
3 C
4 A
5 C
6 B
7 C
8 C

**TASK 5** **Version 2**
The rapid <u>spread</u> of water hyacinths into drainage systems are causing <u>restrictions</u> in the rate of water <u>flow</u>.

**TASK 6**
1  improvement
2  production
3  employment
4  earnings
5  distribution
6  Monitoring

**TASK 7**

| Verb | Nominalisation |
|---|---|
| 1 allocate | allocation |
| 2 consume | consumption |
| 3 create | creation |
| 4 develop | development |
| 5 discover | discovery |
| 6 include | inclusion |
| 7 integrate | integration |
| 8 select | selection |
| 9 separate | separation |
| 10 transport | transportation |

**TASK 8**  Accept any correct transformations.

**TASK 9**
1  [given as an example]
2  *accumulation*
3  *expansion*
4  *changes*
5  *absorption*
6  *drainage*

**TASK 10**
1  a)  Yes – procedure commonly used in experimental research
    b)  Yes – plants of similar size, weight, etc. glass boxes, Nile water, distilled water and wastewater, etc.
    c)  Yes – it gives a lot of procedural information.
2  Past Simple Passive Voice – were collected, were transferred, were selected, etc.
3  Yes. The extract on the next page shows, in **bold** type, the degree of detail offered in the text which should make replication of the experiment possible.

Water hyacinth plant samples were collected from the **river Nile water at Abu El Riesh village (at site, 3×3 m², approx. 1 m deep, 1.5 m from the bank)**, Aswan **city (24°2′N and 32°9′E)**, Egypt in September 1999 and were transferred to the laboratory in **polyethylene bags**. Plants of similar shape, size (**weight of each plant, 200±20 g wet mass**) and height (**roots, 20–22 cm; aerial parts, 26–27 cm**) were selected and washed several times using tap and bidistilled water.

**TASK 11**

1 Three beakers were labelled with these solution concentrations (control, 50% and 100%).
2 The control was filled up with 10ml of spring water with an additional 5ml of Daphnia culture water.
3 Next, the 50% beaker was filled with 5ml of Hudson River water, 5ml of spring water and 5ml of Daphnia culture water.
4 Finally, the 100% beaker was filled with 0ml of Hudson River water and 5ml of Daphnia culture water.
5 After placing the appropriate water concentrations and Daphnia in each beaker, they were stored in a safe and neutral place.
6 Beakers were stored for 1 hour, then 24 hours and concluded in 48 hours.

**TASK 12**

1 Given – 10°40′N, 65°30′W
2 Given – within ten km of 10°40′N, 65°30′W
3 Given – about 1400 m
4 Given – Winds were usually less than 7 m/s, and never exceeded 10 m/s. Seas were usually less than 2 m and never exceeded 3 m.
5 Given – Sunrise barely changed, from 0645 to 0646, and sunset changed from 1820 to 1826 over the course of the experiment.
6 Given – 48 hours
7 Given – Two acoustic measurement sequences bracketing sunrise and two bracketing sunset
8 Not given
9 Assumed
10 Assumed
11 Assumed
12 Given – By listening to the upper 8, 16, or all 32 elements, ideal beam widths could be maintained between approximately 10° and 20° between 20 and 2.5 kHz.

**TASK 13** A good response to this task would be for the student's text to make use of the reader's assumed background knowledge to communicate the main points of the research. The following checklist may help you assess the work.

| The article: | always | generally | partly | somewhat | does not |
|---|---|---|---|---|---|
| assumes the reader is knowledgeable about the environment | | | | | |
| makes use of the reader's assumed knowledge to avoid being boring | | | | | |
| successfully communicates the essential points from the original, explaining concepts where necessary | | | | | |

**TASK 14** Make sure students understand the task. Go through the peer review form with them.

The task recommends 3 peers to give feedback, but this is only a suggestion. The task also works well with 2 peers giving feedback.

**TASK 15** Emphasise the need to be polite, constructive and clear when making suggestions to the writer. Remember that the criteria will vary for different kinds of writing tasks: there are more peer review tasks and forms in Units 8 and 9.

**TASK 16** You should try this out for yourself, preferably with a group of colleagues if you have never done a self-evaluation before: it is harder than it seems, when done thoughtfully.

**TASK 17** Students will need time to go through this process, particularly for the first time.

# UNIT 8 Teaching notes and Key

**TASK 1**
1 Fact      4 Thesis
2 Fact      5 Thesis
3 Fact      6 Fact

**TASK 2**
1 A
2 C, E, F
3 C
4 B
5 E

**TASK 3** **Text A** This text is detailed and descriptive, not argumentative.

**Text B** This text has argumentative style but the questioning tone indicates it is more exploratory than asserting a position: *they might be used; are currently looking toward cloning; They hope …*

**Text C** Several grammatical and coherence clues signal that this text is argumentative. The following items strongly suggest arguments are being weighed and evaluated: *discredits; Rather, particular genes …; In many cases it has been found; yet these traits …*

**TASK 4** The only scope for using argumentative language occurs in the Results and Conclusions sections. For examples, see the italicised text in brackets below.

> **RESULTS:** (*Surprisingly*) In the 1967–69 survey, the ratio of observed to expected concordance for smoking was (*definitely*) higher among identical twins than among the non-identical twins for those who had never smoked (overall rate ratio, 1.38; 95% confidence interval, 1.25 to 1.54), for former smokers (overall rate ratio, 1.59; 95% confidence interval, 1.35 to 1.85), for current cigarette smokers (overall rate ratio, 1.18; 95% confidence interval, 1.11 to 1.26), and for current cigar or pipe smokers (overall rate ratio, 1.60; 95% confidence interval, 1.22 to 2.06). (*We believe that*) The data also suggest genetic influences on quitting smoking. Identical twins were more likely than non-identical twins to <u>both</u> quit smoking (overall rate ratio, 1.24; 95% confidence interval, 1.06 to 1.45).
>
> **CONCLUSIONS:** In this cohort of adult male twins, (*beyond a doubt*) there were moderate genetic influences on lifetime smoking practices.

| Support | Contrast | Conclude | Add weight | Show caution |
|---------|----------|----------|------------|--------------|
| For one thing | Although<br>However<br>however | Consequently<br>Hence | In fact<br>indeed | It would seem<br>While |

**TASK 6** Some of the personal material can be kept, as long as the focus is moved to a more widely-accepted set of views and not just 'my' opinions. As always with written texts, there is more than one way of doing this.

> ~~In my opinion,~~ Becoming a strong writer calls for a blend of inherent ability and skills that are learned. ~~I believe that~~ In my opinion, the 'closed capacities' (Foster 180) are skills that can be trained and that any intelligent person ~~will~~ should be able to master. But ~~I doubt~~ it is less certain whether the 'open capacities' such as good discourse structure and style can be taught or learned. ~~I am often surprised by~~ It is surprising how many people say they have had a writing course and yet still can't create a good essay.
>
> Although ~~we can't prove it yet, it seems to me beyond a doubt~~ it still remains to be proved, my view is that you need more than good skills in the closed capacities to become a good writer. ~~I think~~ It has been argued that people who have learned how to write a clear and accurate five paragraph essay with an introductory paragraph, three main body paragraphs with some support in each, and a concluding paragraph, can definitely learn to develop their open capacities and become good at invention, arrangement/organisation, and self-revision by practice and plenty of reading. ~~I know I did.~~

**TASK 7** (Answers will vary but you should check the accuracy of any suggested answers that are unfamiliar.)

1 Cloning is a technique that makes the replication of a person without sexual reproduction scientifically possible. Scientists have already successfully cloned sheep, hens and other animals.

2 All humans within the range of normal intelligence have the potential to learn to talk. Even children who were brought up without access to human language can learn to talk as long as they are not past the age of normal language development.

3 The availability of universal education is a key goal of the United Nations. The UN funds several significant projects designed to help countries bring education to all the children in that country*.
   *Students can be asked to identify ONE example of a country where this is happening.

4 Research on twins separated from birth shows the importance of the home environment on their personality development. But research also shows that genetics, or the qualities the child is born with, is very important.

**TASK 8**

Table 4. Birth Weight-Specific Perinatal Mortality Rates (PMR) in Singletons and Twins in the United States, 1995–1996

| Birth weight (g) | Singletons | | Twins | | Relative risk |
|---|---|---|---|---|---|
| | Total births | PMR | Total births | PMR | |
| 500–999 | 25.852 | 714.3 | 5.120 | 638.5 | 0.9 |
| 1000–1499 | 51.120 | 364.5 | 10.266 | 298.9 | 0.8 |
| 1500–1999 | 45.968 | 133.9 | 11.288 | 63.5 | 0.5 |
| 2000–2499 | 86.256 | 65.7 | 26.392 | 19.1 | 0.3 |
| 2500–2999 | 296.640 | 19.6 | 58.784 | 6.5 | 0.3 |
| 3000–3499 | 1,212.416 | 5.0 | 61.880 | 3.2 | 0.6 |
| 3500–3999 | 2,830.336 | 2.0 | 25.676 | 3.4 | 1.7 |
| 4000–4499 | 2,238.976 | 1.4 | 3.842 | 4.9 | 3.5 |
| >4500 | 795.440 | 2.0 | 394 | 9.2 | 4.7 |

The highest level mortality rate for singletons
The highest level mortality rate for twins
Where twins have better survival rate.

**TASK 9**  (The suggested text given here is only one of many acceptable possibilities.)

According to Table 1-E there are big differences between food prices in Spain and Germany. Germany's GNP is more than double that of Spain (30,941 : 15,405). However, the cost of food in Spain is much lower than it is in Germany. Meat costs less than half as much in Spain (91 : 187); although the gap is not as wide when we look at bread and cereals, the cost of these items in Spain is still much cheaper than in Germany (89 : 145).

**TASK 10**

The results reported show that the purchasing power of different countries in Europe varies greatly. A family in Denmark or Germany will need to spend much more on bread and cereals than a family in Portugal or Greece. In Austria and Belgium the purchasing power is almost exactly the same. Further, a family in Denmark or Germany will need to spend even more on meat than in Portugal or Greece. Information about Luxembourg was not available. Meat costs are higher in every European country except Spain than in the US. The countries that will find it most difficult to afford meat are Portugal and Greece.

.......................
**TASK 11** (Answers shown in bold italics.)

Previous studies have shown that although, in general, twins have higher perinatal mortality rates than singletons, this is not true in all conditions. This large-scale controlled study investigated whether this paradoxical situation is due to (1) gestational age distribution differences between the singleton and twin populations, or (2) the increased likelihood of birth having occurred in an advanced perinatal centre.

*First*, this study's findings confirm the lower mortality of preterm twins. **Second**, after controlling for level of hospital of birth this difference remained, suggesting that birth in an advanced perinatal centre was not a major factor responsible for the twin advantage. **Third**, the study confirmed previous findings that preterm twins have lower mortality than singletons at the same gestation. *However*, analyses in which gestational age was standardized indicate that, for those whose gestational age was less than 2 SD below the mean for their particular group (twin or singleton), twins were at higher risk than singletons.

*Thus*, the results support earlier authors' suggestions that the definition of *term birth* should be different for twins and singletons.

Adapted from J.C. Payne et al, *Perinatal Mortality in Term and Preterm Twin and Singleton Births,* Twin Research Vol 5, No 4.

.......................
**TASK 12** (The suggested text given here is only one of many acceptable possibilities.)

Future research could investigate the opinions of experts on twin births, including pediatricians and midwives, to see whether agreement might be reached over the realistic definition of *term birth*, that is, the length of gestation when twins are 'ready' to be born. It is certainly clear that the standard *term birth* definition of singletons cannot apply to twins.

.......................
**TASK 13** (Check for answers in bold and those scored through, as shown below.)

Many twin studies (1) **make use of** identical twins (who (2) **have** the same genetic makeup) who were raised in differing environments in order to control for genetic effects: that is, any variation between twins (3) **is** clearly attributable to the environment, allowing the researcher to quantify the effects of the environment by measuring variance of a trait between twins. Identical twins (4) ~~had~~ **raised** separately may have experienced quite different environments; yet many studies (5) **have often ~~been~~ found** that they live similar lives, have similar personalities and similar levels of intelligence. On the other hand, even identical twins who (6) **have been raised** together often differ in significant ways.

http://en.wikipedia.org/wiki/Nature_versus_nurture: Retrieved 21-3-04

.......................
**TASK 14** This is an open writing task and each student will produce his or her own work.

**TASK 15** As we approach the end of the course and the expectations for good writing rise, students should be expected to systematically revise their writing. No-one can write an academic text of adequate quality in one draft. It is often a good idea to collect both the original draft and the revised paper from students at the same time, to get home the message that revision is an important – and natural – activity. With the addition of the criterion, 'Does the text fulfil the task?' to the four we had in Unit 7 – organisation, clarity, vocabulary, and language – it becomes clearer that the criteria here are related to those used in IELTS although they are not the IELTS criteria. When students pay conscious attention to criteria for their writing, they are helping themselves prepare for writing tests as well as helping themselves improve their writing.

You can decide on your own criteria, as long as the students are told exactly what these are before beginning each task sequence. Some kinds of writing will probably need different criteria.

Keep in mind that the four Principles: Clarity, Honesty, Reality and Relevance, are general principles and will help students plan and judge their own writing in a wide range of contexts.

# UNIT 9 Teaching notes and Key

**TASK 1**  1 D
2 B
3 A
4 C

**TASK 2**  (The first answer was given as an example.)

> Situation: girls face educational discrimination – millions kept out of schools.

> Problem: situation improving too slowly.

> Solution(s): make primary education free – countries should adopt innovative methods to help girls stay at school.

> Evaluation: these methods were successful in Bangladesh.

**TASK 3**  Here is the problem (underlined) as stated in the article.

> Since the opening of the first elite private school in June 1992, private schools have mushroomed in China. By November 1996, there were more than 60,000 private institutions, hosting 6.8 million students (China Education Daily, 11/1/1996). Though the percentage of private schools is still less than 4 percent of all schools in China, the current boom in private schools, especially the primary and the secondary level, <u>evokes many debates and concerns over their legitimacy, policy, implementation, problems, and effects (Kwong, 1996). Are these private schools pioneers for quality education or are they a result of an increasingly stratified society? What roles do they play? What are their potential effects?</u>

Accept any reasonable answer that fits the situation.

**TASK 4**  Here is the solution from the original article.

> <u>In response to this experience of mixed results, in September 2001 World Education organized a national meeting of parents' school committees to discuss their experiences related to the subsidy and to propose to the Ministry of Education measures to address these problems.</u>

Accept any sensible answer that fits in with the situation and problem.

**TASK 5**  1  He evaluates it positively.

2  Accept any of the underlined words/phrases below.

Following this meeting, the conclusions and recommendations were presented by the national association of parents' associations (FENAPEB) to the Minister of Education. In fact, this was the first political action taken by FENAPEB, whose members are being trained by World Education with a grant from USAID. Soon afterwards, the Minister of Education issued a policy decree <u>largely based on</u> the FENAPEB recommendations and clarifying the role of the parents' associations in managing the subsidy funds. Since the start of the 2001–2002 school year, this new policy has been applied throughout Benin. Initial indications are that it <u>has helped to settle the situation</u> by providing guidelines on the role of the parents' associations in determining the use of the subsidy.

It has also, it should be noted, given FENAPEB <u>a seat at the table</u> in policy dialogue with the Ministry. Since their <u>initial success</u>, FENAPEB now participates regularly in such discussions, which is <u>an important step forward</u> in building a partnership between government and civil society to manage the educational system in Benin.

[Extracted from http://www.usaid.gov/regions/afr/ss02/benin.html visited 7/11/03]

**TASK 6**  Accept any answer that conforms to the S-P-S-E structure.

**TASK 7**  *Introduction structure*

| Structure | Contains | Sentence |
|---|---|---|
| Situation | The topic and background | The question of parental involvement in schools is a relatively modern phenomenon. In the past, parents sent their children to school and largely left it to the school to educate them as it saw fit. |
| Problem | The nature of the problem | While this arrangement was widely respected, it is no longer a model for educational arrangements today. Nowadays, parents see themselves as providing the finances for schools whether they be private or public and as financiers they are demanding a say in what happens in the schools. |
| Solution | The solution | In order to accommodate this desire for parental involvement, many schools have created parent–teacher bodies and have brought parents onto the school's board of governors. |
| Evaluation | How well the solution works | These moves have gone some way towards giving parents a role in the schools, but there is more that could be achieved. |

········
:······················
:

**TASK 8** Below is the order of the original article. However, since texts can be put together in a number of satisfying ways, you can accept any sensible ordering provided the students can support their choice.

| 1 | The need to improve education in the U.S. has received unprecedented attention recently in the media and in national and state elections. |
|---|---|
| 2 | Prescriptions for improving schools have been many, but two of the most common are what might be called the technology and testing remedies. |
| 3 | The technology prescription proposal holds that placing modern technology into schools will improve teaching and learning and will prepare students for an increasingly technological workplace. |
| 4 | The second prescription, which is often called high stakes testing, holds that standards-based accountability for students, teachers and schools will provide real incentives for improvements in teaching and learning. |
| 5 | What is little recognized, however, is that these two strategies are working against each other because they fail to take the rise of technology into account. |
| 6 | Recent research shows that paper-based written tests severely underestimate the performance of students used to working on computer (Russell, 1999; Russell & Haney, 1997). |
| 7 | The situation is analogous to testing the accounting skills of modern accountants, but restricting them to using their fingers for calculations. |

[Adapted slightly from: Russell M. & Walt Haney. Bridging the Gap between Testing and Technology in Schools. *Education Policy Analysis Archives*. Volume 8 Number 19 http://epaa.asu.edu/epaa/v8n19.html]

········
:······················
:

**TASK 9** Accept any introduction that shows a Situation–Problem structure.

········
:······················
:

**TASK 10** Suggested answers as follows. Note: 'girls' and 'education' were given as examples.

| Repetition of key terms | Meaning relatedness |
|---|---|
| UN report | report/boys/girls/schools/Education for All report/UNESCO/UN |
| education | school/primary school/school fees |
| school | education/girls/primary school/boys/children |
| girls | females/boys/gender/children/them |
| boys | girls/females/children |
| gender | boys/girls/females/parity/equality |

**TASK 11**  Here are some suggested answers. (The answer in italics was given as an example.)

| Coherence strategy | Examples |
|---|---|
| 1 Repeating a word or words from a sentence in the following sentence. | UN report – the report<br>on education – in education<br>seven girls – to outnumber girls<br>primary school – in schools<br>developing countries – populous countries<br>million children – to put children |
| 2 Use a synonym (word with same meaning) of a word from a sentence in the following one. | *prevented from – block* |
| 3 Use a pro-form (e.g. pronoun) in the following clause/sentence. | girls – millions of them |
| 4 Use a sequence marker [e.g. Firstly, secondly/a), b), c)]. | No example in text. |
| 5 Repeat a sentence structure. | No example in text. |
| 6 Use connectives (e.g. moreover, firstly, etc.). | In addition<br>Nevertheless |
| 7 Use a hyponym (e.g. police station → building/car → means of transport). | females – girl<br>school – primary school<br>children – boys, girls |

**TASK 12**  (The first two answers were given as examples.)

Many people assume that democracy is a naturally developing system, and still more assume that (1) **it** has always existed in the United States. This (2) **assumption** is wrong because, as the excerpt below indicates, developing democracy in the United States has been a decidedly difficult and sometimes very contentious matter. The (3) **development** of democracy is an argumentative process, one that requires both time and patience. (4) **Those** who assumed that the newly emerging nations growing out of the breakup of the Soviet Union in 1990–91 would turn to democracy would need to re-examine the history of the United States, or England, or France (or any of the democratic nations of today). A (5) **re-examination** would show that the move to democratize Eastern Europe and Central Asia is just starting and that (6) **such** a movement will require nurturing and encouragement from all sources. Democracy is a difficult system both to institute and to maintain.

Adapted from http://www.globaled.org/issues/177.pdf page 3

**TASK 13**   The answers are underlined. (The first was given as an example.)

1  a) definition
   b) classification
   c) <u>introducing the situation</u>
2  a) <u>reinforcing the situation</u>
   b) contrasting with situation
   c) introducing a problem
3  a) comparison
   b) <u>example of the situation</u>
   c) contrast
4  a) <u>reinforcement</u>
   b) classification
   c) definition
5  a) comparison
   b) <u>a change in the situation</u>
   c) further example of the
      situation
6  a) <u>support for the original
      situation</u>
   b) reinforcement of the change
   c) comparison with 50
      countries
7  a) <u>the problem defined</u>
   b) reinforcing the situation
   c) classification

8  a) <u>recommendation</u>
   b) definition
   c) example
9  a) <u>explanation of problem</u>
   b) classification
   c) result
10 a) example
   b) <u>recommendation</u>
   c) contrast
11 a) making a contrast
   b) <u>giving a reason</u>
   c) showing a cause
12 a) reinforcement
   b) <u>request</u>
   c) opinion
13 a) <u>evidence for
      recommendation</u>
   b) recommendation
   c) contrast
14 a) <u>details</u>
   b) comparison
   c) definition

· · · · · · · · · · · · · · · · · · · · ·

**TASK 14**   (The first answer was given as an example.)
1 D   2 F   3 B   4 A   5 C   6 E   7 G   8 I   9 H

· · · · · · · · · · · · · · · · · · · · ·

**TASK 15**   Ask students to find out what marking criteria are used in their departments. Group students from the same department for the discussion. Groups report to the class. Encourage students to keep a version of their departmental marking criteria and/or a copy of the criteria listed in Task 14, to hand when writing essays.

· · · · · · · · · · · · · · · · · · · · ·

**TASK 16**   ■ Give students time to decide on a number of problems connected with their school systems.
■ Once they have identified the problems, direct them to search the Internet for solutions. Follow this up with a class discussion of the problems and solutions.
■ Then direct the students to write their own essays, individually.

# UNIT 10 Teaching notes and Key

Most of this unit has no 'right answers': we hope that by this stage the students do not need absolute answers, and that they are working out their own needs and solutions.

**TASK 1**

| Para | Key area | Para | Key area | Para | Key area |
|------|----------|------|----------|------|----------|
| 1 | I **M** R D | 2 | I **M** R D | 3 | I **M** R D |
| 4 | I **M** R D | 5 | I M **R** D | 6 | I M **R** D |
| 7 | I M R **D** | 8 | I M R **D** | | |

**TASK 2** You should expect students to be able come up with at least 4 good additional questions of their own. Questions should be:
a) clear
b) not have 2 or more elements [e.g. 'Do you agree that biodiversity is endangered by logging and over-fishing?' is a question with 2 parts and a student might agree that over-fishing causes harm but disagree about logging.]
c) short and simple in order to encourage people to respond to them.

**TASK 3** Expect students to have a fairly short paragraph as this is a very simple survey; no more than one sentence for each of the questions they have collated data on.

**TASK 4** If students have opportunities to discuss the claims and interpretations they want to make with other students (students they have NOT worked with in developing their questionnaire or collecting their data), they are likely to discover any unrealistic, unclear, unsupported or irrelevant claims and arguments they have made.

**TASK 5** Refer to Appendix B for ideas, but make your own decisions on what's important for **your** students in doing this task successfully: the criteria we suggest can only be a general guide for you.

**TASK 6** All show plagiarism.

**TASK 7** One possible answer:
The studies reviewed here indicate that students benefit from feedback during and after writing from peers and teachers.

**TASK 8** Alderson, J.C. & D. Wall. "Does washback exist?" <u>Applied Linguistics</u> 14, 2 (1993): 115–129.

Ferris, D. "Responding to writing." In K. Hyland & F. Hyland. <u>Feedback in Second Language Writing: Contexts and Issues</u>. New York: Cambridge University Press, 2006.

Hamp-Lyons, Liz "Social, professional and individual responsibility in language testing." <u>System</u>, 28 (2000): 579–591.

Hamp-Lyons, L., J. Chen & J. Mok. "Supporting secondary English language teachers and learners: Developing good teaching strategies for giving written feedback on student work; and good learning strategies for effective use of teacher feedback." <u>Report to the Standing Committee of Language Education and Research (SCOLAR)</u> Hong Kong: SAR, 2002.

Matsuda, P. "Second language writing in the twentieth century: A situated historical perspective." In B. Kroll (Ed.) <u>Exploring the Dynamics of Second Language Writing</u>. New York: Cambridge University Press, 2003.

**TASK 9** Alderson, J.C. & D. Wall (1993). Does washback exist? *Applied Linguistics*, 14, 2: 115–129.

Ferris, D. (2006). Responding to writing. In K. Hyland & F. Hyland. *Feedback in Second Language Writing: Contexts and Issues*. New York: Cambridge University Press.

Hamp-Lyons, L. (2000). Social, professional and individual responsibility in language testing. *System*, 28: 579–591.

Hamp-Lyons, L., J. Chen & J. Mok (2002). *Supporting secondary English language teachers and learners: Developing good teaching strategies for giving written feedback on student work; and good learning strategies for effective use of teacher feedback.* Report to the Standing Committee of Language Education and Research (SCOLAR), Hong Kong SAR.

Matsuda, P. (2003). Second language writing in the twentieth century: A situated historical perspective. In B. Kroll (Ed.) *Exploring the Dynamics of Second Language Writing*. New York: Cambridge University Press.

**TASK 10**
a) Use of initials in APA versus full personal name or initials in MLA. Date of publication next to name versus at the end in MLA. MLA underlines title of books and names of journals; APA uses italics.

b) There is not a great difference between the systems. The placing of dates near the front of the reference (APA) perhaps makes it easier to quickly see how up to date a reference is.

**TASK 11**   Paraphrase 1 does not cite the source; it also uses too much of the source language to be considered a paraphrase.

Paraphrase 2 is a better paraphrase, but it is still not acceptable since the source is not cited.

Paraphrase 3 is a good example of paraphrase mixed with selective quotation. The source (Wilson) is cited and could be easily identified in the Works Cited section.

**TASK 12**   A suggested answer:

The paper provides arguments to support the proposition that the internet is making it difficult for businesses to continue to be successful because of its ability to rapidly transfer information. Due to the availability of information competitive advantage does not last very long and usually leads to a price war which is difficult to maintain. To avoid pricing wars businesses can promote their products' advantages in terms of perceptual value.

One such type of perceptual value mentioned is reliability. However it is claimed that this type of advantage is difficult to sustain because of the proliferation of user reports on reliability via chat rooms, forums and usenet groups.

Another type of perceptual value is the notion of overall cost savings where the consumer feels that they are saving in some other way by buying the product. The example given is that one product may be easier to use than another. However, the internet can negate this advantage by providing access to tutorials that make the competitor's product just as easy to use. The article concludes that two options need to be explored: maintaining or reducing price while adding new perceptual values generated through, for example, research and market surveys.

**TASK 13**   **Extract A**

a)  Some of the elements that make this text seem 'alive' are:
  i)   The widespread use of the active voice rather than the passive; 'he found' rather than 'it was found' makes the text easier to follow because it meets our expectation that typically we will read about somebody (a subject) who will do something (predicate) to somebody else/something (the object).
  ii)  The use of the present tense gives a feeling of immediacy/it is happening now, e.g. 'Warren and Edwards (2001), however, <u>find</u> no effect …' and 'Jacob <u>points</u> out, however …'.
  iii) The authors' use of the word 'puzzling' makes them seem more human by introducing an emotional response to the data. This also grabs our attention by positing a puzzle to be solved, 'The discrepancy between the Jacob (2001) and Warren and Edwards (2001) results is puzzling, since both use the same data.'

iv) The authors do not refer to themselves as 'we' in order to focus the reader's attention on their ideas and to make their writing appear more objective. Compare: 'It would be useful to reanalyze the NELS data using Jacob's sample and Warren and Edwards' models' with '**We felt** it would be useful to reanalyze the NELS data using Jacob's sample and Warren and Edwards' models.'

b) A scholarly approach: evaluating the puzzling data and coming to a reasoned conclusion.

**Extract B**

a) i) The use of the personal pronouns 'we', 'she' and 'I' make this text seem populated with real people and highlight the argumentative nature of the text.

ii) The Active voice dominates this text and highlights the subjects of the sentences, for example, 'Watson-Gegeo', 'she' and ' I'.

iii) She is identified in full because she is the main topic of the paper.

b) A combative approach.

**Extract C**

a) The extract opens with a panoramic view of human life everywhere and then focuses in on the beliefs of the two writers.

i) 'We' refers to human beings/people.

ii) 'Our' also refers to human beings.

iii) 'Our' refers to the two writers.

iv) 'We' also refers to the two writers.

**TASK 14** Students should be encouraged to respond in a personal way to the texts and think about those areas that struck them as interesting and useful. For example, they may admire the very even-handed approach of the first extract, or the more combative approach of the second. They may have been surprised to find that academic writers in some fields use the Active voice more than the Passive, and so on.

**TASK 15** The research report should be a substantial piece of work completed to a high written standard. The length should be in excess of 2000 words.

# Appendix A Tips for carrying out peer review

When reviewing, it is always important to note a paper's strengths, so that the author will not lose these in the process of revision.

Never assume your peer will automatically know which parts of a paper work well; many people find it easier to read and comment on someone else's work than to see the strengths and weaknesses of their own work. Often we are too 'close' to our own work to see it clearly. The peer review form asks you to list the three major strengths of the paper – but if there is time, try to do this throughout the paper too, writing marginal comments like 'good paragraph' when you read a part that flows well. Even a smiley face can encourage your peer!

*But how to deal with the parts that really do have problems?*
The key is to make sure the comments you write are substantive comments.

As we read, we all have reactions to problematic parts of a paper: 'Huh? This is unclear' 'Gosh, this is disorganized!' 'What is this person trying to say here?'. But these reactions are only the first step in the process of making helpful comments, and writing down these initial reactions as comments is not very useful to the writer.

*How can you turn these unhelpful comments into helpful ones?*
You need to go a step beyond your initial reaction, and ask yourself why you are reacting negatively to that sentence or paragraph. Why, for instance, does a paragraph seem disorganised? Are several topics mixed together in one paragraph? Or is a single topic dealt with, but presented out of logical sequence, so that the reader is constantly grasping for information not yet given? Or does the writer seem to start with one idea or point of view, but then reverse this later in the paragraph?

You can see that this process will take some work on your part, because you need to reflect on your reactions and read your peer's writing in a very involved way. Below are some examples of unhelpful 'reaction-type' comments that have been turned into helpful comments by this process of reflection.

### Example 1

Unhelpful comment: 'This section needs work.'

Helpful comment: 'Can you combine the related actions into a single sentence, and make sure all the parts focus on Methods?'

### Example 2

Unhelpful comment: 'Disorganized!'

Helpful comment: 'This section discusses 2 things: Can you separate each into its own paragraph?'

### Example 3

Unhelpful comment: 'These references are not relevant.'

Helpful comment: 'I think you need more references from people who have shown whether and how different ways of teaching affect students' learning, and less on other things that are not part of your focus, like class size or intelligence.'

### Example 4

Unhelpful comment: 'Unclear.'

Helpful comment: 'Does the experiment show that the way of teaching made a difference, or not? Which are you concluding?'

# Appendix B  Academic writing assessment criteria

<table>
<tr><th colspan="5">Academic writing assessment criteria</th></tr>
<tr><td>Criterion</td><td colspan="3">Quality</td><td>Comments</td></tr>
<tr><td></td><td>Very good</td><td>OK</td><td>Needs much work</td><td></td></tr>
<tr><td>Genre</td><td></td><td></td><td></td><td></td></tr>
<tr><td>The writing fits into the usual expectations for academic writing that is done for the purpose stated for the task</td><td></td><td></td><td></td><td></td></tr>
<tr><td>Ideas</td><td></td><td></td><td></td><td></td></tr>
<tr><td>The paper contains enough material to satisfy the reader on the topic that is being addressed<br><br>The content is clear and relatively easy to understand</td><td></td><td></td><td></td><td></td></tr>
<tr><td>Organisation</td><td></td><td></td><td></td><td></td></tr>
<tr><td>The introduction clearly focuses the reader's attention on the purpose of the text</td><td></td><td></td><td></td><td></td></tr>
<tr><td>The text is well arranged in paragraphs, and the ideas are well arranged within each paragraph</td><td></td><td></td><td></td><td></td></tr>
<tr><td>The last paragraph summarises or concludes the paper clearly</td><td></td><td></td><td></td><td></td></tr>
<tr><td>Everything in the text is relevant</td><td></td><td></td><td></td><td></td></tr>
</table>

| Research (where relevant) | | | | |
|---|---|---|---|---|
| Clear evidence of research Appropriate use and acknowledgement of sources | | | | |
| **Style** | | | | |
| The level of formality is suitable for the intended reader | | | | |
| The writer is able to use a variety of sentence types that suits this writing task | | | | |
| **Mechanics** | | | | |
| grammar, spelling, punctuation | | | | |

# Appendix C  Assessing written work

People write for many purposes, and so do students. Not all those purposes are formal, and not all are to be assessed. We recommend that courses focusing on teaching writing should similarly include writing that is not to be assessed, and writing that is to be assessed less or more formally. We have often indicated within each unit what assessment approach we think would be appropriate for a task or a particular stage of the course. The underlying principle is that few tasks are to be formally assessed, but that students should have plenty of opportunities to get feedback of all different kinds.

## Formative feedback

'Feedback' is the responses that a person receives when they take part in a communicative activity. Feedback on writing can be spoken or written, and it need not only take place after the writing has been done. Feedback given early on, when the person is thinking of ideas to write about, can be very stimulating and useful. Feedback given at different stages of the writing process is useful for different reasons, and different writers will respond differently to the feedback they receive.

A major controversy about feedback concerns whether it should be in the form of *correction* or *commentary*. In our opinion, both commentary and correction have a place, and teachers can experiment to find out which works best for which students and at which stages of writing. The answer will not be the same for every student. It is easy to see, however, that neither correction nor commentary is of any use unless students have the chance to *revise their writing*. Only by revising can writers make practical use of the responses they get from the teachers or their peers; and only by revising can writers try out what they learn from error corrections. Without a revision stage in the teaching and learning of writing, teachers might as well save their own time and simply put marks on writing, with neither comments nor corrections. But we do not recommend this!

### Stages of formative feedback

Three 'stages' of formative feedback are suggested here, which differ in the amount of information they give the student as opposed to the amount of self-correction they expect of them.

### a) Correction

In this stage, the student's errors are clearly identified on the paper, and they are corrected by the teacher, as in the following example.

Britain can exchange their [*its*] ideas to [*with*] ~~the~~ different countrys [*tries*]. They also helps ~~to~~ the underdeveloped countries. Britain is make friendship [*making friends*] with other countries through this programme. Britain can ~~able to~~ distribute here [*her*] modern techniques of feeding and breeding of livestock to the different ...

Correction permits the learner to see exactly what was wrong and how it should be written, but it leaves no work for the learner to do.

### b) Controlled correction

In this stage, the student's errors are clearly indicated – but not corrected – by the teacher. Instead, the teacher helps the student to correct their own errors by stating in the margin what type of error they have made, as in the following example. (Note, refer to page 210 for the key to correction marks.)

*delete article* Britain the studying engineering
in Britain is so ᵛadvantageous.    *repeated subject*
These things are avaliable ˢ because
Britain is one of the industrial countries, and
*sx2* labrotary equipments are avaliable ˢ
at any institution in Britain.

Controlled correction give students plenty of support, and also leaves them with some work to do, in self-correction. The correction activity helps learners to remember the correct forms and avoid the same errors in future.

### c) Guided correction

In this stage, there are two possibilities: either the locations of errors are pointed out but the student is not told what types of errors they are; or the number and types of errors are indicated but the student is not told exactly where they are. Both approaches guide the learner toward self-correction but require care and thought from the student if the error is to be satisfactorily corrected.

   You can see both types of guided correction in the following examples.

v     we can easily get familiar with the real needs
      of practical industries.
         In addition to these advantages we can obtain
?m/v  the way how they find the clue of new technologies
P     and how they think and how they solve the problem.

The measures to be taken <u>caused</u> an excessive
change resulting in some serious proble<u>m</u>.
   Firstly, we lost, <u>senic</u> beauty of mountains, rivers,
grassland etc, which are essential to our mental
health. We rush to <u>the limited area</u> and an
over<u>crowd</u> leads to further destr<u>action</u> of nature.

---

Correction key: Most teachers want to develop their own
system or code for students' errors, depeding on the specific
recurrent problems which they identify, but the following system
is simple to use and simple for students to understand.

---

**s** = spelling
**c** = concord (agreement: subject and verb)
**s/p** = singular/plural
**w/o** = word order
**T** = verb tense
**v** = vocabulary, wrong word or usage
**app** = appropriacy (inappropriate style or register)
**P** = punctuation (including capital letters)
**Ir** = irrelevant information
**?m** = meaning not clear
**^** = word(s) missing
(J. Willis Teaching English Through English)

For teachers who are looking for a more detailed way of providing
their students with formative feedback, the 'Formative Feedback
Profile' on the next page will be helpful. A profile like this allows the
teacher to indicate for each individual writer what their weaknesses
are in specific areas. For example, a writer may be 'Excellent' on *Ideas
and Organisation* but only 'Adequate' on *Surface features* due, perhaps,
to problems with handwriting. There are so many possible
combinations using the Profile that every writer in a class could
easily get a different Profile: this makes the feedback to the student
really personal. By keeping a copy of the Profile every time it is

completed, as well as giving a copy to the student, the teacher is able to keep a record of each student's progress over time.

Teachers wishing to make multiple copies of *page XX* (the Formative Feedback Profile) for the purpose of providing feedback to their students need not obtain further permission from the authors or publisher.

### Formative feedback profile

| Communicative quality | Excellent | a pleasure to read |
|---|---|---|
| | Very good | causes the reader few difficulties |
| | Adequate | communicates although with some strain |
| | Fair | conveys its message with difficulty |
| | Weak | does not adequately convey its message |
| Ideas and Organisation | Excellent | completely logical organisational structure; effective arguments and supporting material |
| | Very good | good organisational structure; well-presented and relevant arguments and supporting material |
| | Adequate | clear but limited organisational structure; some arguments unsupported or material irrelevant |
| | Fair | logical breakdowns apparent; ideas inadequate and/or poorly organised |
| | Weak | logical organisation absent; no suitable material |
| Grammar and Vocabulary | Excellent | wide range and fluent control of grammatical structures and vocabulary |
| | Very good | effective use of an adequate range of grammatical structures and vocabulary |
| | Adequate | adequate range of grammatical structures and vocabulary, but could be used more effectively |
| | Fair | restricted range and uncertain control of grammatical structures and vocabulary |
| | Weak | grammatical structures not mastered and limited range of vocabulary |

| Surface features | Excellent | handwriting, punctuation and spelling show no faults |
|---|---|---|
| | Very good | occasional faults in handwriting and/or punctuation and/or spelling |
| | Adequate | handwriting and/or punctuation and/or spelling could be improved |
| | Fair | definite weaknesses in handwriting and/or punctuation and/or spelling |
| | Weak | little mastery of the conventions of handwriting or punctuation or spelling |

(Liz Hamp-Lyons *Formative Feedback Profile* 1986)

## Summative feedback

Summative feedback is more often known as 'marking or 'grading', or even 'testing'. While formative feedback is based in the classroom, on what students are doing, practising and learning in the classroom, summative feedback is based outside the classroom. Summative feedback is primarily used to inform, by *summarising*, how far a student has progressed towards meeting the expectations of a course or a programme of study. It is the type of feedback that is usually placed into student records, on report cards or in test results and, while it can be useful to the writers and the teacher, it is probably more useful to authorities who need to look at larger-scale issues such as how (and whether) a whole class, school year or school district, is progressing. Once summative feedback has been reported on a writing task, a sequence of writing or a course, there is no longer anything the writer can do to improve their writing and therefore improve their mark/grade.

The actual judgements made for summative purposes are usually based on the same criteria as have been used for formative purposes during the course; but instead of being reported descriptively to students (as illustrated in the Formative Feedback Profile on p.211), summative judgements are usually reported in marks (such as 8/10; 9/20; 65%) or grades (such as A–; B; C+). Formative systems can be converted to summative use by attaching a number to each step on the scale (for example, Excellent = 5; Very good = 4; Fair = 2) and, if there are several different scales or groups of criteria (such as Organization + Grammar + Punctuation), the number on each different scale or criterion can be added together, as shown below.

| | |
|---|---|
| Communicative quality | 4 |
| Ideas & Organization | 3 |
| Grammar & Vocabulary | 4 |
| Surface features | 3 |
| **Total** | **14/20** |

And this figure can be converted using the system adopted in your own context.

It is important to realise that judging writing is difficult, and that it is subjective – a matter of (usually informed) opinion. Summative judgements are often influenced by factors such as how far the student was interested in the task or the specific topic; by handwriting; by the teacher's awareness of whether the student has worked hard or been a bit lazy. To be fair to everyone, these summative judgements should be based on several pieces of writing and not just one or two. They should also be based on a range of topics, task types, genres of text, different length requirements and conditions (at home, in class, a short timeline or a long one, with and without opportunities for peer discussion, feedback and so on). Because everyone varies in how well they write depending on many factors, we can get the most accurate (which is the fairest) approximation of their 'real' writing ability by judging as widely as possible and averaging out the results. For summative purposes it is also a very good idea to work with a colleague and have two or more of you judge the writing. Responding to and judging writing is a personal thing as well as a professional skill, and several teachers' summative judgements give a better idea of how the writer's writing is valued by teacher-judges as a whole.

Remember, too, how important it is to explain to students why they got a particular score or grade, and to make sure that summative and formative feedback work together to help students understand their own strengths and weaknesses and how they can make progress.